RUMI

EDITED AND TRANSLATED BY

GEOFFREY SQUIRES

MIAMI
UNIVERSITY
PRESS

RUMI

POEMS

FROM

THE

DIVAN-E

SHAMS

LIBRARY OF CONGRESS CATALOGING-IN-PUBLICATION DATA

NAMES: JALĀL AL-DĪN RŪMĪ, MAULANA, 1207–1273, AUTHOR. |
SQUIRES, GEOFFREY, TRANSLATOR.

TITLE: RUMI : POEMS FROM THE DIVAN-E SHAMS /
EDITED AND TRANSLATED BY GEOFFREY SQUIRES.

OTHER TITLES: DĪVĀN-I SHAMS-I TABRĪZĪ. SELECTIONS. ENGLISH

DESCRIPTION: OXFORD : MIAMI UNIVERSITY PRESS, 2020. |
INCLUDES BIBLIOGRAPHICAL REFERENCES AND INDEX.

IDENTIFIERS: LCCN 2019024833 | ISBN 9781881163671 (PAPERBACK)

CLASSIFICATION: LCC PK6481.D6 E5 2020 | DDC 891/.5511—DC23

LC RECORD AVAILABLE AT HTTPS://LCCN.LOC.GOV/2019024833

DESIGN BY CRISIS

PRINTED ON ACID-FREE, RECYCLED PAPER
IN THE UNITED STATES OF AMERICA

MIAMI UNIVERSITY PRESS
356 BACHELOR HALL
MIAMI UNIVERSITY
OXFORD, OHIO 45056

PREFACE

Rumi is the only poet I know of who has three different names. He was born near Balkh in Afghanistan so the Afghans claim him and call him Balkhi. He wrote mainly in Persian so the Iranians call him Molavi or more formally Molana, meaning 'master'. After travelling through Iran to Baghdad and Damascus in Syria the family finally settled in that part of Turkey which had been part of the eastern Roman empire; hence Rumi. This westward movement was driven mainly by the need to keep ahead of the Mongols who were spreading south and west in their second major invasion of the region.

After Rumi settled in Konya in Turkey he became a well-known and widely-respected religious figure and teacher who exhibited a scholarly but profound interest in Sufism, the mystic tradition within Islam. This interest initially came from his family background and was developed through formal study in various centres. Then one day a wandering dervish called Shams-e Tabrizi walked into his life and turned it upside down both emotionally and spiritually. Shams was in some ways his alter ego, wild where Rumi was restrained, rude where Rumi was civil, extreme where Rumi was moderate: someone whom Rumi's students and followers distrusted and even hated. However, the *Maqālāt* (Discourses) of Shams show that he was also a source of intense spiritual insights rather than simply a wild card: see the translations by Chittick (2004) and Fouchécour (2017). The relationship between the two, which involved at least one temporary absence on the part of Shams, lasted twenty months, at the end of which time Shams disappeared finally without trace.

The ghazals—short lyric poems—translated here comprise a very small sample from the massive collection—over 3000 ghazals and many quatrains also—which Rumi composed, often accompanied by music and dance, during their time together and after Shams's departure, which left him distraught. They tell the story of that strange encounter and the *bouleversement,* the over-turning, of Rumi's whole existence, and in so doing take us deep into the mysteries of Sufism.

RUMI

1

O sudden resurrection
infinite mercy   love that knows no bounds

fire spreading through the groves of thought

today you came laughing like the key to the prison
to us wretches here like grace from heaven

condition of hope   sun's chamberlain
seeker and sought   conclusion and beginning

rising up in the breast   adorning the mind
you create the need   and fulfil it then

2

A sweet-lipped one brought news
that a caravan had arrived from Egypt
a hundred camels laden with sugar and candy
Lord what bounty

like a candle lit at midnight   or a spirit re-vivifying a corpse

I asked   what do you mean
she said   you-know-who has come
my heart leaped
it made a ladder of the intellect
and scaled the roof through love
looking for proof of this news
and suddenly saw there   a world beyond our world
a limitless ocean in a jug
heaven in the form of earth

and sitting on the terrace a king   dressed as a watchman
a spacious garden   a paradise
in the breast of that gardener
the image transmitted from his breast to mine
manifesting the heart of that king

O image of him never leave my sight
that my heart may be revived for a time

Shams of Tabriz has seen that placeless place
and made a world of it

3

That moon   which the sky never saw   even in dreams
has returned
bringing with it a fire no water could extinguish
look at the dwelling of my body   look at my soul
the one insensible   the other laid waste
by the cup of his love

when the tavern-keeper became my soul-mate
my blood turned to liquor   heart to skewered meat
when the eye fills with his image   a voice resounds
bravo the goblet   well done the wine
and when my heart espied love's ocean   suddenly
it plunged in   abandoning me   and saying
find me now

the face of Shams-uddin   glory of Tabriz
is the sun   in whose pursuit   hearts race like clouds

4

My sun my moon has come   my eyes and ears have come
that silvery breast has come   that seam of gold has come
he who turned my head   the light of my eyes   has come
whatever else you care to mention   that too has come

that highwayman has come   the wrecker of vows has come
that Joseph with the jasmine body   is suddenly by my side
today far surpasses yesterday   O faithful friend of mine
last night I was drunk out of my mind   when I received the news
that the one I had been searching for   high and low with a lamp
had crossed my path   come into my hands   like the tight bud
of a rose

5

That face that form   movement his alone
as if the moon came walking in a gown
that colouring   that teasing look
stature cheek and hand and foot

should I speak of the cypress or the verdant meadow
tulip or jasmine
should I speak of the candle or the chandelier
or the dance of the rose in the gentle wind

O love burning like a fire-temple
that came to me in this image   this form
pillaging my heart's caravan
give me some peace
afire and aflame am I from night till dawn

in the countenance of this morning sun
lie all my triumphs my good fortune
and I circle his face   luminous as the moon

wordless I salute him
meekly laying my head upon the ground
before he even speaks

6

I have sat myself down at your door
so that haply your promise to me
might finally be fulfilled
like a kettle comes to the boil

so that you might open the door
saying   arise come in
I sink down here on the threshold
half-drowned in your amber and musk
may a hundred thousand blessings
be upon your lovely head
now and forever

I am drunk   out of my mind
detached from the affairs of men
for all I care the world can go to ruin
as long as your love remains
for when your love claps its hands
a hundred new worlds are made
a hundred centuries
out of the skies   out of nothing
O my love who smiles like the rose
whose gaze is like perfect knowledge

all that can be known
O my cavalier of the sun   like *Hal Ata*

today I am your guest
intoxicated by your laughing countenance
when I speak of your face
God knows my heart leaps

where is there a terrace like your terrace
a name like your name   a cup like your cup
O my gentle cup-bearer

if I found someone with a living soul
I would seize his garment by the hem

I dream of dreaming   and seeing your face in my dreams

7

You are the sun and like shadows
things cannot but follow you

sometimes to the left   sometimes to the right

8

His two gazelle-like eyes would capture lions
from them a hail of arrows falls on me
the bow of his brow and darts of his eyelashes
bear witness he is the emir of my soul
and if I am confused
by the confusion of his hair   not by his hair
it is because it surpasses musk or amber
if my soul twists and turns and cannot get free
it is because my heart is chained up in that dungeon

say not that there is the equal of our cypress
for the beauty of our moon is beyond compare
I lay my head down before him   though for him
my life is nothing   but a trivial thing

kneel down before the image of the king
for that image itself is a vizier to the Real

9

Go friends and catch my love and bring him here
bring him for once and all
that idol always ready to slip away

with sweet songs and gilded pretexts
bring me back here that luminous countenance
that bright moon
and if he promises to come   in just a moment
that is only a trick
he is trying to fool you

for with his warm sentiments
he can get away with anything

his words do so charm and bind
he can conjure knots in the waves
can truss up the air

and when finally he enters   to blessings and joy
sit down and behold God's marvel

with his beauty what price the beauty of the lovely
while the sun of his face extinguishes the lamp

O heart   go fleet-foot to Yemen to my beloved
carry my greetings and vows to that priceless jewel

10

I have laid another trap   so that I may capture him
he who slipped through my hands
the one to whom my heart is prisoner
if I have to spend the rest of my life
I will get him back again

for my heart has melted like sugar
and my liver is congealed in pain
and my sight will not be restored
till I have sight of him again

I shall make my way to his place
at night by the light of his face
and when I get to his alleyway
I shall grasp the ring on his door
for my heartache grows ever worse
my face will be as pale as gold
and when he goes to take that gold from my face
I shall grab him

I am racked with suffering
how could it be worse than this

if I am turned upside down no matter
upside down I will capture him

till dawn I shall wait for him
he will be like putty in my hands
I shall loosen the cord of his gown
I shall get hold of his belt

for his eyelids have begun to droop
quickly I shall come from behind
he has started on the road towards sleep
I will catch him on the bend

11

I saw from a distance Shams-uddin
pride of Tabriz envy of the Chinese
eye and light of heaven
he who gives life to the earth
each person who has witnessed such a being
becomes who they really are and more

he demanded who shall I kill cruelly
and I replied
ambush this humble slave
we conversed like this then suddenly
he loosed an arrow from a hidden bow
incinerating the existence of this servant
pulling up my arrogance and my hate
his heart is not black like that of the tulip
but the cup of his wine renders the jasmine drunk

the very purpose of things lies in the folds of his gown
he has blessed us this king
shaking his sleeve over us
and when he shows his face to the moon
he saddles the steed of the firmament

12

Wherever you go you are with me
you are my two eyes my light
if it is your wish get me drunk
or if you wish annihilate me

this world is like Mount Sinai
and we like Moses are seekers
at every moment comes a sign
like a flash of lightning
cleaving the mountain in twain
one part turns green the other white as narcissus
one part the colour of pearl the other like ruby and amber

O you who want to behold him
lift up your eyes to these hills

O mountain
what nature of wind blows upon you
for we have become drunk on its sound

13

I used to be the nation's favourite ascetic
lord of the pulpit
but fate turned my heart
into a lover
clapping his hands ecstatically for you

14

Happy the time we sit in the porch you and I
two forms two faces one soul you and I
the garden and the sound of the birds
like some immortality upon which we have entered

the stars come and stare at us
and we point out the moon itself to them
you and I without any you or I
at one is this joy

how remote we are from the fables and the babble
of this world   you and I
even the parrots of heaven have become
gourmets of sweetness in this place
where we smile in the knowledge   you and I

and this is the strangest thing   that while we remain
here in this corner we are simultaneously
in Iraq   Khorasan   you and I
assuming one image here and another there
in that timeless paradise and sweet domain   you and I

15

Whoever asks you about the *houris* of paradise
proffer him your cheek and say   like this

whoever speaks of the moon
climb up on the roof and say
like this

if anyone seeks a fairy show him your face
and if anyone mentions musk
shake out your hair and say
like this

if anyone asks you how the clouds reveal the moon
undo your gown knot by knot and say
like this

if anyone asks you how Jesus raised the dead
kiss me on the lips in front of him and say
like this

and if anyone asks about those who are slain by love
show him my soul and say
like this

16

O Shams
what are we to make of the heart
which sometimes settles in love and sometimes flees it

17

O with me and hidden as the heart   heartfelt I greet you
you are my Ka'aba   wherever I go I turn to you
wherever you are you are here   keeping my door
even from afar
and at night my house lights up if I think of you

sometimes like a tame falcon I beat my wings in your hands
sometimes like a soaring pigeon I sing the song of your dwelling
if you are absent why do you trouble my heart constantly
and if you are present why do I need to detain you

you are a long way off
but from my heart to yours there is a tiny window
and like the moon secretly I send you messages from there
O light that sends your light to me   from afar

soul of all the forsaken   my soul is enslaved by you
my heart is a mirror which I polish for you
and my ears are the book in which your kind words are recorded

18

I was drunk and my heart abandoned me
it fled from me   but where
when it saw that the bonds of the mind had snapped
it left   fleeing   in ecstasy
it will have gone nowhere surely
but to the seclusion of God

do not look for it in the house
for it belongs to the air
it is a bird of the air   it is in and of the air

it is the white falcon of the emperor
it has taken off and flown to the emperor

19

I have committed no crime other than
to want you in my heart
why then do you turn your face away
from the pallor of mine
either show some kindness to
the travails of this broken heart
or give it the strength to bear
God does what he wills

the road divides
patience   or grace granted
as a reward for what one has done
without the light of your face
I can find neither

was dust ever seen
except in the rays of the morning sun

O when you turn away
all streams run dry

20

That friend who turned up last year   kitted out in a red tunic
resplendent as the moon
has returned this year sporting a rust-coloured gown

that Turk whom you saw as he set about pillaging
is he who has come back this year   looking like an Arab

the friend is one and the same
though the clothes are a different hue
he changed his coat then headed back
the wine is genuine even though the flagon is new

see how he has returned
giving great pleasure to our circle of drinkers
O comrades   you thought that flame was mortal
but it has emerged once again through that secret portal

21

In the alleyways of love the cry goes up
a window has opened in the house of the heart
giving light to all

what window

since the light of your sun has come
there is no shadow left the width of a needle

22

I stand before you each hour   and wither and grow again
but how could anyone raise with you the case of a single soul
when a head springs from the dust wherever your foot has trodden
how could anyone renounce you for the sake of his own head

the day when the soul takes off   at the pleasure of your scent
it knows   does it not   the fragrance of the beloved
and the moment the brain begins to purge itself
of that intoxication
each hair on the head laments   and a hundred sighs emerge

I have emptied my house   to fill it with your things
I have diminished myself   so that your love might grow
my soul pursues your love   O Shams al-haq
footless   like ships over the sea

23

The heart is like a grain
and we are like the mill
how should the mill know
why it turns

the body is like a mill-stone
the mind like a rushing stream
the stone thinks
the stream understands

but the stream refers you to the miller
as being the one
who arranged its fall

the miller responds
you have bread to eat
where would the baker be
if the mill did not rotate

and so on and so on
be silent
ask God so he can say

24

Everyone has eaten and fallen asleep leaving the house quiet
so now is the time for us to take a turn in the grounds
to effect an introduction between the apple-tree and the peach
and relay a few words from the dewy rose to the jasmine

spring-time is like the Messiah performing a miracle
with the winter-martyrs of plants throwing off their winding-sheets
and since those sweet-lipped idols have now opened their mouths
he who does not get a kiss may still get drunk on their breath
and the glow upon the cheeks of the tulip and the rose
tells me there is a lamp hidden somewhere behind all this

the leaf trembles on the branch and my heart is trembling too
the leaves tremble in the wind like my heart for the charms of
Khotan
the light breeze spreads the fragrance with a gentle hand
teaching the children of the garden how to comport themselves
the wind of the holy spirit blows like the spirit upon Mary
see how bride and groom sit together holding hands
when the cloud espies them beneath their canopy
it scatters over them jewels and pearls from Aden
and now that the red rose has rent its skirt with joy

the time has come for Jacob to be given the shirt of his son
and when the Beloved's lips laughed   like a carnelian from Yemen
the scent of the divine came to Mohammed from that land

we have spoken much about this and that   but our hearts have not found rest
except from the spreading tresses   of the true king of our time

25

How would it be if my love   took me by the hand tomorrow
leaning through the lattice window with the disc of his moon-like face
if he who adds life to my life untied my hands and feet
for my hands and feet too have been bound by separation
I would say to him O beloved   without you   O life of my soul
pleasure gives me no happiness   and wine does not fill me with joy

and if he responded playfully saying   get away
what do you want of me
I fear that your melancholy   would make me melancholy too
I would bring him sword and shroud   as if for a sacrifice
saying if I give you a sore head   prepare to cut mine off
you know that without you I have no wish to live
and I hereby swear by God   who brings back to life the dead
it is better for me to die   than to live apart from you
I never thought for a moment   you would turn your back on your
  slave
believing these were the slanders and lies   of my worst enemies
you are my soul my existence   the very life I lead
you are my vision my eyes   and without you I cannot see

O minstrel cut short this verbiage   and play us a melody
bring your lute and tambourine   if you do not have your reed

26

Like the rose I laugh with my whole body
not my mouth alone
because I am without myself and with
the king of the world alone

O you who brought a torch
and carried off my heart at dawn
despatch my soul after my heart
do not take my heart alone

do not let my soul
become estranged from my heart
out of rage or jealousy
do not leave the one here
and call for the other alone
send out a royal summons
issue an invitation
how long O sultan shall the one be with you
and the other remain alone

and if you do not come
and seal my lips tonight

the way you did last night
I shall emit a hundred cries
O you who constitute my life

I will not lament alone

27

Gather together friends   for this is no time to sleep
every member who is asleep   by God
is not a true companion

he who is not turning and groaning
like a waterwheel
will not see the face of the garden
or find his way to it

you who seek your heart's desire
in this world of water and clay
are as mad as someone who searches for
a dried-up stream

come down from the sky of the heart   O moon
and turn our night into day
so that no traveller may say
this is a moonless night

may my heart remain uninformed
as to the world the Beloved inhabits
if it does not tremble like quicksilver
for love of him

28

This house which continually resonates
to the sound of shaker-bells
ask of its master what kind of dwelling it is

if it is the Ka'aba
why is there the visage of this idol
and if a Magian temple
how come the light of God is shining here
there is a treasure in this place
too great for the universe to contain
the house and its master
are simply constructs   fictions

do not lay hands on it
for it is a precious talisman
and do not address the master
for he has been drunk
all night long
the dust and dirt of the house
are nothing but ambergris and musk
and the sounds that emerge from it
nothing but poetry and song

in sum

everyone who enters the house

has found his way

to the Sultan of this land   the Solomon of his times

29

You claim
day and night I perform the prescribed prayers

how is it   O brother
that everything you say is not a prayer

30

Listen to the heart's intimations
without words
and in not understanding understand

in people's stony hearts there is a fire
consuming everything that is not real
and when all those veils have been consumed
we come to understand the stories of *Khezr*
and the *knowledge from Us*

then in the heart and soul appears
the ever-new face of that ancient love

when you recite *behold the sun*   behold the sun
and when you recite *lam yakon*
behold that gold-mine

31

Come closer   O come closer
my faithful friend
forget about you and me and come the more quickly

come closer and leave behind you and me
so that there is neither you nor I
forget your arrogance your pride and in its place
assume your true majesty

He said *Am I not* and you answered   *yes*
what thanks is there for that *yes* but tribulation
what is the secret of that yes   only that I
beat on the door of poverty and annihilation

leave   do not leave that place
what is that place   and whereabouts its threshold
cleanse yourself   reduce yourself to dust
so that out of your earth   flowers may grow
and when in the end you wither   burn happily
so that your burning may give out light
and if after burning you are nothing but ash
that ash will form the philosopher's stone

which leads back to the invisible
which created you out of a handful of dust
which out of the spray of the sea created land
and with dark smoke painted the sky

which makes of a mouthful of bread the basis of existence
and transforms that living breath into consciousness
offer yourself to this master   this great plan
for it is when it gives its own life
that poverty is most generous
and if you devote your days to proving your faith
you will get in return a life that is boundless
and filled with happiness

I have said enough and will be silent
for it is in silence
that the speech of the soul truly finds its voice

32

What mitigation O my heart for all these faults
on his side such faith on yours such faithlessness
on his side such largesse while on yours
such moderation such parsimony

he is so delicate and you so crass
with you such jealousy such fantasies
and dark imaginings
with him such taste such allure
such munificence

why such taste so that
your bitter soul might become sweet
and why the allure if not to draw you in
to the company of the saints

you are ashamed of your sins
and have the name of God upon your lips

at that moment he draws you in
so that he may save you

33

When I see your form in the mirror I start to speak
but my breath clouds the mirror so I can say nothing
when I see you in the water I reach down
but the water is disturbed and I can do nothing
my friend I have no friend here
if I want to say 'my love'
I cannot utter your name
I have closed my mouth   I have stopped myself
sending my cries back the way they came

34

The rational person is always at pains to flaunt
his rationality
the lover by contrast is beside himself
out of his mind
the rational person is cautious steers clear of the ocean
loving by contrast is all about drowning
the rational person finds comfort in creating comfort
the lover is ashamed at the very idea
even in a gathering the lover remains distinct
oil and water together do not mix
if some reasonable person offers advice to the lover
his only reward is mockery and derision

love smells of musk and that is why
it is notorious
how could it ever escape this reputation
love is like a tree and lovers its shadow
though the shadow be long it must have an origin
to become wise the child must grow into an old man
old men who fall in love become young again

O Shams whoever abases himself to love you
through your love will become exalted eminent

35

Do not seek me in this world or the next
for those two worlds are lost in the world I am

36

Your love took away my chaplet   and gave me couplet and song
much praying and repenting did I do   but my heart did not hear
at love's hand I became a poet   clapping my own hands
your love consumed my righteousness   and everything I possessed

I used to be as chaste   and steadfast as a hill
but when your wind blows   hills are swept away like chaff
if my slopes echo with sound   it is the sound of your voice
and if I am only chaff   in your fire I turn to smoke

when I beheld your existence   I was shamed into nothingness
and out of love of nothingness   the world of the soul was born
whenever nothingness comes   our being is diminished
but when it came to me   praise be   my being was increased

37

Of these two thousand ones   I wonder   which one am I
listen to these murmurings   do not cover my mouth
and since I am senseless do not leave a glass in my path
for if you do I shall tread on it   everything I find I break
because at every moment my heart is confounded by your image

if you are joyful I am joyful   sad I am sad too
if you are bitter I become bitter   kind then I am kind
how good it is to be with you   O my idol
of the sweet lips   delicate chin
you are the original
I am but a mirror in your hand
whatever you are I become   like your faithful reflection

were you a cypress standing in the meadow
I should be your shade
in the shadow of your flower   I have pitched my tent there

38

O you who have set off on the pilgrimage
where are you where have you got to now
come come the beloved is right here

the beloved is your next-door neighbour
with only a wall between you
so why are you wandering in the desert

if you see that faceless face
you will become at once
the Lord the House the Ka'aba
ten times you have made the journey to that place
come inside it this once and climb on this terrace here

according to you that house is beautiful
but give me some idea of its master
if you have been in that garden
bring me one bunch of flowers that you have picked
and if you have swum in God's ocean
show me the pearl of one soul
as proof

O that your trials and tribulations
might be turned into treasure
alas that you hide that treasure from yourself

39

If you break my harp   O lofty one
there are still thousands of other harps here
since I have fallen into the clutches of love
how can I feel deprived if I have no harp or reed
if all the world's harps and rebecks were burned
many a hidden harp would remain   my friend
the plucking and twanging of them rises to the heavens
even if it does not reach the ears of the deaf

if all the world's lamps and candles were to go out
it would not matter since we still have iron and flint

songs are like spray upon the face of the sea
no pearl rises to the surface but I tell you
the grace of the spindrift derives ultimately from the pearl
it is the reflection of the reflection of that gleam
which bathes us in its light

songs are only an expression of the yearning for union
root and branch   origin and manifestation
are not at all the same

close your mouth and open the window of the heart
for that is the way that we can converse with spirits

40

I am free of lust and desire
alive or dead they are a calamity
dead or alive
the grace of God is my only country

I am free of this verse   these lines
O king and sultan of eternity
this rhythm of tee-tum-tee-tum-tee-tum
that has half-killed me
let all these rhymes and sophistries
be swept away
for they are nothing but dry husks
round the kernel of poets' thought

O silence
do not depend on the mind
which veils all that is most marvellous
rely less on intelligence and learning
for in silence there is neither fear nor hope

41

The beloved is all the lovelier
in this cold and rain

the beloved in one's arms and love in mind
the loved one in one's arms and what a beauty
gentle and supple and fresh as a young shoot
in this cold let us hurry to his place
for no mother ever gave birth to one such as he
in this snow let me kiss his lips
for snow and sugar both refresh the heart

I have no strength left
I have lost control of myself
having been carried away and back again
when his image suddenly enters my heart
my heart leaps

O God is great

42

For you   I have given up my life
for your sake I have put up with wounding tongues
I have listened to burning taunts
and been pierced by arrows from those self-same bows

if I present my heart to you
you will forgive me   seeing the signs of blood

if an enemy speaks ill of me
O master
being my enemy   what else could he say

43

This idol spends the night
teaching love-tricks to Venus and the Moon
and with the spell of his eyes
binds up the two eyes of heaven

O Muslims   look to your hearts   since with me
my heart has become so involved with his
I no longer have one I can call my own

to begin with I was born of his love
in the end I gave him my heart
like when fruit grows on a bough
it hangs there

I flee from my shadow because
my shadow hides the light
what rest can there be for one
who flees his own shadow

the tip of his hair says   here
do the rope-trick   climb
and the smile of his candle asks
where is the moth then

be brave   take hold of the strand
coil yourself
and when the flame is lit
throw yourself into it

and once you have known
the ecstasy of burning
even if you are brought the water of life
you will not quit it

44

You have me by the ear   where are you taking me
tell me what is in your heart and in your mind
what did you cook up for me last night   O my dear friend
God only knows what kind of project love is

since the sky and stars and earth are in your grasp
where are they going
if not the same place as you summon me
you have them by one ear but me by both
from the roots of which I cry   long life to you

when the slave gets old his master sets him free
but when I got old my slavery was just beginning
will not the little children arise with white hair
on the day of resurrection
but with your rising
old men have dark hair once more

since you revive the dead
and rejuvenate the old
I shall be silent and devote myself to prayer

45

Union with the beloved   or drinking with friends
if you cannot get to the ocean   dip your foot in the stream

those friends who like the soul   are eternal beings
fellow-travellers of running water   generous as a shower of rain
companions of the Water of Life   the *Khezrs* of the skies
the life of every building   treasure of every ruin

water is the intimate of light   the one pure   the other shining
each one tells tales   not out of spite but goodwill

a hand disturbs water   in the cup or the pool
and the light   it also   trembles on the wall

see the marvels   O my brother   of the origins of nature
I will shut up   see for yourself   it is He who knows all

46

Once more the violet stands by the bending lily
once more the ruby flower has torn its blouse
once more they have come like the wind
as if from the other side of the world
our dancing happy drunken friends dressed up in green

the flag-waving cypress has put autumn to flight
and the sweet-faced anemone graces the mountain-tops
the hyacinth bids the jasmine good day
and the latter replies salām to you too
welcome to the meadow young man

everywhere the Sufis celebrate
clapping their hands like poplars   dancing like the morning breeze
the bud like a veiled woman hides her face
but the wind lifts the veil exclaiming
O pure one   show yourself

our true friend has come to our street
water fills our channel
with such morning glory   why remain thirsty and pale

mean-faced winter has gone   that kill-joy has been killed

47

When I am sober I am quarrelsome
apt to take offence

but when I am drunk
what patience   what silence

48

O sleep I implore you do not afflict us tonight
for God's sake do not pass by here tonight
there where you fly over the meeting is ruined destroyed
do not fly over this gathering tonight

tonight our sight has been magnified by his beauty
O eyes do not regret that you cannot close
when the night envelops us
O sleep begone stay alert
so that you may receive a hundred gifts
from those wakeful hearts

if everyone has slept O heart give thanks to God

if you did not sleep much last night
you will do so even less tonight
with the moon as my companion I shall talk until day comes
O friend of lovers the night will bring you insight
into what is

the moon has become my witness with an army of stars
O moon be my shield against the arrows of the stars tonight

49

That red rose which rips its cloak
I know where it is coming from
and the willow that hangs straight down
to atone for the prayers it has missed
and the lily with its sword   the jasmine with its shield
who each swearing by God
prepare to wage holy war

the wretched nightingale   sighs at the rose's display
each bride in the garden says   the rose is beckoning me
but the nightingale replies
it is poor me
importunate from head to foot
whom the rose is doing this for

the plane tree raises its hands pleading
shall I tell you what it prays for
who put the bud's hat on   who bent the violet double
although the autumn was harsh indeed
see how spring has kept faith
what autumn stole from us   spring has reimbursed once more

when I recount these things
the beauty of the garden   the roses and the nightingale
it is only an analogy
to show the ardour of love
its zeal
or explain the grace of God

for the pride of Tabriz and the world
has shown me favour again

50

You are lighter than a breath of wind
no one is full of you or tires of you
O my soul
who could weary of you or have enough
you are that breath of which God said
it will revive the dead

the mouth of the tomb will open
and swallow you in one gulp
when your body's mouth closes on the breath of existence

give me more air   so that my lungs may fill
like a goatskin water-bottle
and with your breath I may sail over the seas
may the day never come when you stop breathing
for then no plant will flourish in the fields

O save your breath   for you have another one
when this one grows faint   the other will take its place

51

When the proprietor of the bath-house   what a moment
emerges from his private quarters
all the paintings on the bath-house wall
prostrate themselves

all these figures   frozen lifeless unconscious
at the sight of his eyes
open their own as wide as a narcissus
through his ears their ears
fill with fables
and through his sight they can see far and wide

you can see each figure drunk   dancing
like a companion who every so often
plunges into the pool of wine
and the bathhouse rings with their noise and cries
as if it was the day after the day of judgment

laughing they call to one another
from one end to the other
but none of them can see where the proprietor is
because they are all running here and there

excited confused   looking for him
while he is in front of them and behind them
incognito

that king of souls at the head of his army

52

I have a physical form
for you to give life to
you are the soul of the soul of the soul
and I the bodily mould

53

Before there were any gardens grapes or wine
in this world
we were drowsy on the wine of eternity
in the Baghdad of the realms of the spirit
we announced *I am the Truth*
before Mansur's claim the judgment and the gibbet

before the Architect created this earthly realm
we were ensconced in the tavern of the divine
our souls like the universe wine-cups like the sun
so that with the wine of the spirit
this turning world was everywhere bathed in light

O serving boy ply with drink
these self-satisfied creatures who have feet of clay
so that each of them realises
just how remote they are from that true state

54

For the lover and the thief
the night is spacious and long
come harlot night and do the work of both

I steal carnelians and pearls
from the sultan's treasury
I am not so niggardly
as to steal some draper's cloth

under night's veil   delicately
the thief finds a clever way
to scale the roof of the house of mystery

I have no aim other than
through darkness and trickery
to find the king's treasury
and steal the precious carnelian of his charm

55

O Shams of Tabriz   let the stream flow
so that the water-wheel may turn the mill

56

There was no favour which that face did not bestow
what did we do   if he did not grant you favours
you rail because that lover was a tyrant
but in heaven or earth
whoever saw a beauty that was not

his love was sweet though he did not give us sugar
his beauty constant though he was not faithful
show me a house that is not filled with his lamps
or a window that does not show his lovely face

this eye and that lamp are two separate lights
when they come together none can distinguish them
when the spirit became lost in wonderment it said
no one has contemplated the beauty of God but God

each of these metaphors is at once
an explanation and a distortion
and as to *the morning splendour*
even God is jealous of his own creation

the sun of Shams' face   the glory of Tabriz
never shone on the transient but made it eternal

57

Like a mirror my soul displays its secrets
I am able not to speak   but unable not to know

I flee the body   but hold back from the soul
I swear I do not know
whether I am this or that

58

He is a meadow to which all flowers flee for shelter
for in him there is no autumn   in him leaves are not shed

he is a fine and stately tree in the middle of the desert
in whose shade one might fall asleep and wake up tipsy

he is a sky like the heavens   whose purpose is to befriend the soul
where Saturn does not intrude to quarrel with Venus

he is a jewel of grace in that placeless place
from him comes a sign to the heart   like two tear-drops falling

59

Although the Mongols have destroyed this world through war
why should I be concerned
since the ruins conceal your treasure

the world might be broken but you
are the beloved of those who are broken

60

O do not despair if the beloved turns you away
if he sends you away today will he not welcome you tomorrow
if he closes his door on you do not go
wait there
for if you are patient
in due course he will usher you
to the seat of honour

and even if he bars all the roads and paths
that lead to him
he will show you a hidden way which nobody knows

61

Come for you are the very soul of the dance
come for you are a swaying cypress
in the garden of the dance
come for there was never one like you
nor will there be
come you have no equal in the spectacle of the dance
come for the spring of the sun rises
out of your shadow
come for you are a thousand Venuses
in the heavens of the dance
the dance expresses its gratitude to you
in a hundred eloquent ways
all I want to say is a couple of things
about the significance of the dance
you will be beyond the two worlds
if you enter into the dance
for the world of the dance
lies beyond this world or the next
be the terrace of the seventh heaven ever so high
it is far surpassed by the ladder of the dance
stamp under your feet all that is not it
for the dance belongs to you and you belong to the dance

62

Well now
look where all our companions
have laid their heads down
love's wine has taken effect   they have fallen asleep
love's fever has opened their gowns
they have removed their hats   undone their belts

and all these cries these fights these arguments
for what
are they not fellow-travellers on the road
part of the same caravan
have they not all the same provisions
for the journey

63

I was dead and came to life again
weeping then laughing
love's government arrived
empowering me forever

my eyes have seen their fill
my soul has been emboldened
I have a lion's heart
like Venus I shine bright

he said you are not insane
are not worthy of this house
I went off and went mad
returning thus in chains

he said you are not drunk
you are not part of this party
I went off and got drunk
coming back again merry

he said you have not been slain
you are not bloody with joy
in front of his life-giving face
I became lifeless was struck down

he said   you are far too clever
for your own good
drunk on doubts and illusions
I turned into a fool
free from all that

he said   you have become a candle
the whole focus of this assembly
but I am not part of this gathering
I am nothing but wisps of smoke
that rise from its burning

he said   you are a sheikh
a leader and mentor for our band
I said I am not a sheikh
but a slave at your command

he said   you already have wings and feathers
so I will not give you these
but because of my desire my need
I became like a flightless bird

new fortune arrived and said
do not be sore   do not go
for out of grace and benevolence
I am coming to you now

and ancient love said to me
stay here close to my breast
I agreed and will remain
here in this place   steadfast

64

I always had some holy book
in my hands
till love gave me shaker-bells
and where my mouth was filled with praise
now there are rhyming couplets
and poems and lays

65

Man makes plans but does not know his fate
human projects do not mirror the will of God
when man thinks ahead it all seems clear
but whatever he tries it is God who decides
he takes a few paces straight ahead
but he does not know where they will lead

seek the kingdom of love   do not waste your breath
for there you will escape the angel of death

66

Who treats the pain for which there is no cure
who is the companion on the endless road
if reason exists then what is madness
if the soul exists then who is the soul-mate
if the light that lights the world eternally
is neither faith nor disbelief   then what

67

For that king who has no call for drums or standards
I have gone mad
and there is no writ that covers
those who are insane
from a distance I appear like a wayfarer
but this is an illusion   there is no one there at all

become nothing
for nothingness is the gold-mine of the soul
but not that soul which is only grief and care

I without I   you without you   let us dive into that current
for this dry land is nothing but grief and oppression
though we drown ourselves in that river
we will not lose our lives
for it is the water of eternal life
and nothing but mercy and grace

68

My heart like a pen came into the hands of the beloved
so that tonight for example it writes Z
and tomorrow again R
he sharpens it to execute one kind of script or another
or to copy some text
the pen says I submit to you as you know who am I
anyway
sometimes he blackens its face now scratches his hair with it
sometimes he holds it upside down now grasps it properly
to use it

on one sheet he crosses out a whole world decapitating it
while on another
he rescues a conjunction from oblivion
oh yes
the status of the pen derives from that of the writer
whether it is in the hand of a sultan or the fist of some general

he splits the nib for reasons he knows best
like Galen knows best what is good for the patient
the pen cannot bestow praise of its own accord

neither can it criticise off its own bat
whether I call it a pen or for that matter a flag
it is both aware and unaware   conscious yet unconscious

the mind cannot grasp or describe it
for it involves a union of opposites
a composition that does not compose

what a paradox
at once determined yet free

69

Do not spend the night-time sleeping   for night is worth thousands of souls
and at night the full moon bestows on us countless rays
from the sky of this world each evening comes down
the army of divine grace to aid those who are suffering

God said   *Arise in the night*   and this was not in vain
for it is her nightly vigil that gives Venus her radiance
the darkness of the night gives insight to what I write
when you cook in the obscurity of night
O you who have much to learn
you are using Moses' fire
the ink of night assists the pen with its knowledge

O Majnūn take in your arms   the Leyla of the night
for night is the sanctuary of oneness   by day idolatry is rife
for Leyla is of the night and the day Majnūn
the light of the wisdom of dawn is to be found in her curls

it is only in the shadows that one finds the Water of Life
what sort of a fish are you   to deny yourself that stream

it was from a black cloth that the covering of the Ka'aba was made
that which gives succour and support to those who submit to God
and inside the Ka'aba of night one prayer is worth a hundred
clearly such a temple was not made for slumbering
that which has no equal   for grace and beneficence
has smashed all the idols in the darkness   so that God alone
    remains

be silent now   and cease
for poetry is of little interest   and ignorance even less

70

What hidden sweetness in an empty belly

man is no more nor less than a lute
for if the belly of the lute is full
no plaint high or low will issue from it
but if your brain and stomach burn with fasting
at every moment a lament will come from your breast
you will consume a thousand veils with that fire
and climb up a thousand steps in your zeal

empty your belly and wail like the reed
when it is a flute
and reveal the mysteries when it is a pen

but if your belly is replete on the day of judgment
you will bring Satan instead of reason
an idol rather than the Ka'aba to the occasion

when you observe the fast
good habits will congregate around you
like slaves and servants and your retinue

observe the fast for that is Solomon's ring
his seal
do not hand it to the devil and destroy your kingdom

71

It is not lovers themselves who search
in all the world there is no seeker but he
this world and the other are made of the same stuff
in reality   in truth
there is no religion nor unbelief nor faith

O you who have the breath of Jesus
do not breathe a word about distance
I am indentured to he who is not far-sighted

if you say 'I shall go back' do not do so
for there is no way back
and if you say 'I shall go ahead' do not say so
for there is no way forward

cling on to what you have
and do not look to others
for the dressing for your wound is the wound itself

all dervishes are a mixture
of good and bad
whoever is not is not a true dervish

whoever leaves his place   his place is his heart
in all this world there is no home but the heart

72

When my beloved's face grew angry
my heart said   what if he is angry with me
I passed through a hundred desert valleys
thinking sadly
what help is there   since my help has turned to this
I flew up into the heavens like a demon
but pain had transformed my heavens into earth

they said to me   follow the straight path
but what way can I take   since my one true guide has gone
my beloved is my way and my companion
his face is both my faith and my religion

73

Reason says   I shall charm him with language
love says   be quiet   beguile him with the soul
the soul says to the heart   get away
do not mock yourself or me
what is there that he does not have
so that I can entrap him thereby

he is not sad or full of care   or has some death wish
that I might overcome with potent wine
I cannot present the arrows of his look with a bow
since the dart of his glance does not require a bow
he is not a prisoner of this world   bound to this earth
such that I could tempt him with gold and dominion
he is an angel though in human form
and is not lustful so that I could entice him with women

angels flee from the house where this icon is
so how could I charm him with such shapes and forms
since he flies on wings he does not need troops of horses
since light is his food how could I offer him bread
he is not some merchant or trader so how could I attract him

with the thrill of profit and loss
he is not some turbaned doctor so that I
could pretend to be ill and win him with my cries

hair by hair he unpicks my dishonesty
since nothing is hidden from him
how can I suborn him with what is hidden
he does not seek fame or renown and is not
like some princes are entranced by poets
so how could I charm him with my flowing lines

how could I engage him with the idea of paradise
or of God's mercy
since the glory of his mysterious form is so great

but Shams-e Tabriz his beloved his favourite
perhaps I could win him with that pole-star of the age

74

However high I go   he is at the summit
when I look for the heart   it is he who carries it away
when I sue for peace   he is the mediator
when I go to war   my dagger it is he
when I go to a party he is my food and drink
when I walk in the garden   my jasmine it is he
when I go down the mine he is my ruby
when I plunge into the ocean   my pearl it is he
when I cross the desert he is my oasis
when I ascend to the heavens   my star it is he
when I am patient he is my counsellor
when I burn with pain   my censer it is he

75

What a banner what a flag
there is no God but God
raised before time began
there is no God but God
how the king like Moses creates
particles of dust
out of the sea of being and nothingness
there is no God but God
and that quality of purity born of humility
that he showed him in pre-eternity
there is no God but God

one injustice of his is better
than a hundred thousand cases of justice
I salute his excellent tyranny
there is no God but God
everywhere he casts his gaze
a thousand Edens grow
there is no God but God

one dramatic day I shall reach the shore
of this sea of suffering
on the waves of his mercy and gentleness
there is no God but God

and anyone you see
whose soul is still sorrowing
has not caught the scent of my king
    there is no God but God

when eyes will not accept collyrium
from that king of Tabriz
what terrible sadness and regret
    there is no God but God
my heart and soul shout out
are you not
to a thousand cries of *yes*
    there is no God but God

such a paradise of grace
of that illustrious prince   Shams-uddin
what a marvellous remedy for suffering
    there is no God but God
my heart like a bosom friend circles around
that forbidden inner sanctum of Tabriz
    there is no God but God

how special it would be for me to say
who is it at the door
and for him to reply
it is me
    there is no God but God

76

When we occupy the centre   he goes to the margins
but when we are beside ourselves   he moves centre-stage

77

Do not seek earthly joy
only the joy in your own heart
which is a veritable mine of sweetness

O God free my soul from those two guards
let me sleep a deep sleep with the Companions of the Cave

grief is the shadow of joy   and runs after it
do not think only about joy
for the two are never separate

grief follows joy   as night follows day
once you see daylight   there is no avoiding night

so long as you embrace sorrow   joy will attend you
but if you look only for joy
grief will be your road   exacting its toll

remember always that crocodile which will devour us
leaving neither imagination nor understanding
beauty nor ugliness   wet nor dry

we will be like a little wax candle
melted down by its own flame
or a piece of paper covered with shapes and images
that has fallen into the stream

78

You ask how is it
that ideas come to us
well think of sleep and that unpicks the knot

79

The road by which I came   which one is it
so that I may return
for everything I do here is vain

to spend even one moment
away from the beloved's thoroughfare
is forbidden in the religion of lovers
if there were a single person in this village
who understood
by God one sign would be enough
but how can a mere goldfinch escape
when even the Simorgh is caught in this complex snare

O errant heart   do not venture here
stay there where you are secure
choose those sweetmeats which best nourish the soul
and find a full-bodied wine
for the rest is only scents and colours and show
conflict and fame and reproof

be quiet   sit down
for you are drunk   and stray near the edge of the roof

80

Have you heard that sugar has got cheaper
in the town
did you know that winter has disappeared
and the good weather come
did you know that in the garden
the basil and the carnation
are laughing behind their hands
because things have suddenly got easier

have you heard that the nightingale
has returned from his journey
has joined in the performance   becoming leader of all the birds
did you know that the branches of the trees
have heard the good news about the rose
and are waving their hands

did you realise that the soul
has become drunk on the cup of spring
and gone off dancing to the sultan's hareem
did you know that the anemone's cheeks are now blood-red
and that the rose has been appointed chamberlain
of the household

have you heard
that when the law officer of spring turned up
thieving December made itself scarce again

these beauties have got passes from the authorities
to make the earth green   dressed up from head to foot

if these princes of the garden performed miracles
at last year's resurrection
this year is a hundred times lovelier

81

And he is with you means
he is with you in the search
so when you search   search for him too

he is closer to you than yourself   so why look beyond
like melting snow wash away your self from yourself

in love a tongue grows in the soul
like a lily
silence your tongue and imitate the lily

82

A hundred times I told you   take care
do not go too far
with these taunts these quarrels   this hostility

on the lute of fidelity and affection
if you play with a plectrum play gently
you know   how could you not know
when one plucks too hard   the strings break

83

With you   life   living
without you   death   annihilation
for you are the sun of all things
and without you the world is frozen

on this chessboard
people are like pieces in your hand
it is you who arrives at check-mate
or takes a few pawns

he said   what will you give me
I who gave you breath
I who will not be unaware
of the day of your death

I prostrated myself before him
like the bent neck of a camel
he laughed and smiled and said
straighten up

look at yourself
what do you think you are doing
you have stretched out your neck
as if to eat cotton

84

That form which nature has made straight
in the end will become as bent as the vault of heaven
but that form which love has made straight
in the end will be higher than the empyrean throne

be silent
for he who knows the secrets of the world is here
he has said
I am closer to you than your jugular vein

85

Life goes by in our expectations of tomorrow
oblivious to disasters to come
today is the only day you have   think
to what use was it put   wasted
in pursuit of profit or pleasure

with every breath we spend our purse of time
death carries off all beings one by one
and the fear that it inspires
makes the thoughtful man grow pale

death lurks near the roadway   waiting
while the gentleman proposes
to take a stroll in the country

86

If you are not a seeker   you will seek with us
and if you are not a minstrel   you will play with us
if you are as rich as Qārūn   love will render you poverty-stricken
if you are a lord   you will become a slave with us

one flame in this gathering ignites a hundred flames
whether you are dead or alive   you will come to life with us
your feet will be unbound   the light will shine out from you
till your whole body is laughing and blooming   like the rose with us

for once dress like a poor man so that you may see those living hearts
throw off your satin robes   and clothe yourself in rags like us
when a seed is scattered a tree will grow from it
when you grasp this secret   you will be sown like us

Shams al-haq of Tabriz says to the bud of the heart
when you open your eyes   then you will see like us

87

Love does not lie in scholarship or learning
is not to be found in books or their pages
whatever people discuss
that topic is not love's way

you must grasp that love's bough
existed before the beginning
and its roots lie in what comes after the end

this tree does not rest on the empyrean of the heavens
or on this earth
it has no trunk or bough
we have deposed reason and set limits to passion
for such reasoning and behaviour
do not merit such respect
so long as you lust   you lust after some idol
when you are loved there is no place for lust

the sailor stands continually
on the deck of hope and fear
when sailor and deck go down
there is only drowning

O Shams you are both the ocean and the pearl
for your being is nothing but the secret of our Maker

88

I shall keep quiet now and shut my mouth
for I am an old man
with a handful of spiteful people for company

89

My verse is like Egyptian bread
leave it overnight and you can't eat it
have it while it is still fresh
before the dust settles on it

its place is the warm climes of the heart
in this world it dies of cold

like a fish for a moment it quivers on land
then a moment later you see it is dead

if you want to believe it is fresh when you eat it
I tell you
you will have to use your imagination

and what you drink is really in the mind
that is not some old wives' tale   my friend

90

Once more you are determined to leave
once more you have made your heart as hard as iron
do not extinguish the light of our friendship
for you have poured oil into our lamp

by Allah   with your countenance
you have filled this world
with roses and lilies and eglantine
by Allah   let no enemy of mine accuse you
of being an enemy while you posed as a friend
by Allah   keep all your servants united
you who have brought light to the world

once more you have set aside
the love-games we used to play

by Allah   you have cleansed the skirts of the evil spirit
with your whirling dance
your shaking sleeves

O gold-mine of royal mints   Salah-uddin
you have made a harvest of silver like the moon

91

Pining for you my heart has become
a melancholy house
in search of you it has gone everywhere
my heart will look upwards   always up
till I quit this carpet of sorrow
and ascend to that beautiful ceiling

but today what has become of it
last night what did that person say to it

in search of that pearl it is as if my love
beat wave upon wave like the sea in my heart

day comes   night's veil is rent again
and my heart still pursues that vision of loveliness
it is only a step from your heart to mine
but what a long road all the same

alas for this heart   alas   alas
seeking compassion
O Tabriz   in my desire for Shams-uddin
how long will my heart journey
to the Pleiades

92

Shame on the people of this world
shame
sons of bitches   imposters   idiots

they give the appearance of ascetics
but inside   there is no room for piety
in that abode

for a few coppers you can get
two or three ass-loads of these quacks

93

At every breath the voice of love comes from left and right
we are going out to the fields to show ourselves to all
the turn of the house is over the turn of the garden has come
morning breathes content with the beloved's face in sight

arise O king of the age wake from your deep sleep
mount the charger of happiness it is time to meet up again
we beat the drum of promises and clear the way of the sky
your joy is turned into cash forget about tomorrow

the army of the day has put that of night to flight
the world high and low is purified and bright
happy the one who escapes this earthly world of the senses
for beyond these colours and scents are the colours of the soul
and heart

O happy that heart that soul who escapes this water and clay
even though the philosopher's stone is contained in pottery

94

Come closer to me   you whose countenance
is nothing but light
who does not languish here for love of you

no   I am mistaken
in the search of one soul for another
do not come   do not go away
for there is no such thing as distance

where do the rays of the sun not shine down
and who does not know the splendour of the moon
thought has no veil but thought
abandon that thought that does not veil itself

O sweetness beyond the imagination of the fly
O honey that does not come
from the honey-bee
the person who still sorrows now
after seeing this moonlike face   has no excuse
each loveless heart   be it a king's
is merely a silk winding-sheet   a tomb

95

It is late   it is late   and the sun has gone into the well
arise O you with the lucky stars   for it is time for the moon to rise
O servant boy fetch the wine   watchman go up on the roof
begone my unquiet soul   for my private love has arrived

the tear which stings the eyelid   the patience which lets life's harvest
  burn
that wisdom which teaches the way   at midnight all go astray
those souls with that inner light are now lighting up the heart
and night   that black Indian slave   announces that our Turk
has now re-entered his tent
that that moon   is back inside its halo again

96

Every image you see takes its form
from that placeless place
if the image vanishes it is not a problem
since its origin is eternal
every face you see   every utterance you hear
let not your heart be troubled if it goes
for it is not so
since the spring is eternal the stream is constant
neither can fail   so why should you lament

think of the soul as a spring
and everything else as flowing from it
as long as the spring remains the stream will flow
dismiss sorrow from your mind
keep drinking that clear water
and do not worry about it running out
for it is limitless

from the moment when you came into this world of being
a ladder was placed in front of you
so that you could climb out
first you were mineral then vegetal

and from that you became animal
how could you not understand this
and from that you evolved into a human being
with knowledge rationality and faith
see how complete this body
which emerged from a dust-pit
has now become

and when you move on from being human
assuredly you will turn into an angel
and beyond this earth your place will be in the sky
pass beyond the angelic realm and dive into that ocean
so that the drop of your existence may become a sea
a hundred times greater than the sea of Oman

instead of the 'son' invoke the 'one'
with all your soul
for even if the body has aged   who cares
the soul remains young

97

Of all the world I have chosen you alone
so is it right that I should sit here grieving
my heart is like a pen held in your hand
it is up to you if I am joyful or cast down

what can I be except for what you will
what do I see except for what you reveal
sometimes you make a thorn of me sometimes a rose
sometimes I emit scents or pick thorns out

if you want me this way I remain like this
if you prefer me that way I become that
in that jar in which you keep the tincture of the heart
who am I what kind of love or hate

you were the first and you will be the last
make my end better than my beginning
when you are hidden I am an infidel
but when you appear I rejoin the faithful

what do I have that you have not given me
what do you want from my pocket or my sleeve

98

Hush

although we might be love's meanest slave
like love we wait in ambush

99

Let us be true companions
sitting at one another's feet
O friends come closer
so that we may look into one another's faces

in our inner being we have many things in common
not only what is visible on the surface
now that we are seated together
with wine in hand and roses concealed about us

100

O God give the minstrels honey
make their hands like iron for the drums
since they have devoted their hands and feet to love
make them true
since they have filled our ears with the good news
grant them a hundred eyes and the blessed vision
to see God
and since they cry out like amorous doves
grant them out of your goodness a sure tower

because in your praise and eulogy
they have created beauty
praise them
and since they have freshened our souls with melody
let them forever have water
from the rivers of paradise

I shall be quiet   O generous one   for it does not need me
to say   give this   grant that

101

You die and behold the world of the soul
and if afterwards you come back to life
you understand what it is to live then
each one like Idris who dies and returns
has taught the angels and sees into what is hidden

come tell me by which road you left this world
and likewise which way you came back
it is that way which souls fly off each night

each night
in town after town the cages empty of birds
when their feet are tied they cannot fly away
soar to the heavens and wheel in the sky
but when in the end through death
they break the ties and ascend
they come to know reality
and the secret of all things

say nothing   stay dumb
silence is plenitude

do not beat the tambour of speech
for the word is an empty drum

102

In the two worlds   O my soul   I have found no joy
except for you
I have seen many wonders but none like you
they say that hell-fire is the infidel's lot
except for Bu Lahab I have seen
none spared your immolation

often I have put the ear of my soul
to the little door of the heart
I heard much talk but no lips did I see
you bestowed your mercy on this servant
all of a sudden
but apart from your boundless kindness
I could see no reason

O my chosen serving-boy   my eyes have fallen upon
no one like you in Arabia or Iran
be generous with that wine which has never been served
at any festive gathering
in that glass the like of which
I did not come across even in Aleppo
bring me jugs of wine
in such measure
that I may lose myself
for in being and selfhood I have known only fatigue

103

There is no limit to this desert
no place of rest for our hearts and souls
world upon world have taken on
different images and forms
which of those images is ours

if on the road you see
a severed head
rolling towards where you are
inquire of it the secrets of the heart
for from it you will be inducted into
the nature of the mystery

how would it be if there were a human ear
that understood the language of the birds
how would it be if some bird took off
having round its neck the collar of Solomon's seal

what can I say   what do I know
for this story lies beyond contingency
the limitations of our human being
yet how can I keep silent
when at every moment my anguish grows and grows

104

Since my sun and moon have transcended shape or form
happily I progress from one reality to another

I am lost in meaning   it is sweeter like that

I shall not return to forms nor contemplate
this world or the next
I dissolve into meaning so that I may become
one with him
for reality is like water and I am like sugar in it

no heart tires of the life of the soul
so I will not hark back
to this mundane world of shape and form again

105

By the time the intellect
has found a camel for the *haj*
love has ascended the Mount of Purity

106

Someone announced   Master Sanai is dead
the death of such a master is no small thing
he was not chaff to be blown away by the wind
he was not water which froze in winter-time
he was not like a comb which broke on a single hair
he was not a seed that lay buried in the earth

he was a cache of gold
in the midst of this dusty plain
for he valued the two worlds as worth no more
than a barley-corn
he discarded his physical body on the earth
and bore his mind and spirit up to heaven

that second soul of which most people know nothing
he committed   I speak in riddles   to the beloved
the pure wine mixed with the dregs
rose to the top and was separated from them

O my dear friend   on this journey
those who hail from Marv or Rey   Byzantine or Kurd
cross paths

and each goes back to where he first came from
what has silk got in common with cotton from Yemen
be silent now   like a compass pointing
for the King
has wiped your name from the book of words

107

I am a painter   a creator of images
time and again I depict some beauty
and then in front of you I have it destroyed
I construct a hundred forms and give them life
but when I see your form   I throw them in the fire

you are the vintner's boy
the enemy of sobriety
he who knocks down every house I build

the soul dissolves in you   mingles with you
since it takes on your scent I shall cherish it
every drop of blood I spill says to your dust
I am the colour of your love   the object of your affection

in this dwelling of water and clay
my heart is desolate without you
O beloved enter the house   or I shall go

108

I was that day when names were not
when nothing in existence had a name
through me names and the named came to be
that day when there was neither I nor we
the tip of the beloved's curl
was to become a sign   a revelation
but the tip of that lovely curl was still not then

I surveyed the Cross and the whole of Christendom
he was not on the Cross
I went to the pagan temple   the ancient shrine
there was no trace of him in either
I looked high and low
in the mountains of Herat and Kandahar
but he was not there
I made my way laboriously up Mount Qaf
but all I found there was the nesting-place of the Anqa
I pointed the reins towards the Ka'aba
but in that destination of young and old
he was not to be found
I asked Avicenna about him

but he was beyond his ken
I went to the scene of the *two-bow-lengths distance*
but he was not present in that exalted court

I gazed into my own heart
I saw him in that place and nowhere else
aside from Shams-e Tabriz he of the pure soul
no one was ever truly drunk or crazy
in this world

109

In the end

get back to the roots of the roots of the self
get back to the roots of the roots of the self
get back to the roots of the roots of the self

110

At dawn a moon appeared
came down from the sky and fixed me with its eye
like a falcon which takes a bird while it is hunting
then picked me up and flew away

when I looked
I could no longer see myself at all
for by the grace of that moon I had become a soul
and while my soul travelled I could perceive only that moon
until the eternal mystery was revealed

the nine spheres of heaven
all folded into that moon
and the little ship of my existence
was entirely submerged in that ocean

that sea became waves and consciousness arose
and with it speech   this is how it was
the sea threw up spray and with every fleck
something took shape and human form
and every drop that had a sign from the seas
dissolved straightaway and became immaterial

without the sovereign saving grace
of Shams-e Tabriz
one could neither see that moon nor become that sea

111

I have heard that you mean to travel   do not go
that you will give your affection to a new companion
do not do so
you may be a stranger in this world
but why estrange yourself
which heart-sore victim do you fancy now
do not steal away from me and go
to someone you do not even know
do not think I have not seen your sidelong glances

O moon who overturned the heavens
you have turned my life upside down as well
where is the pledge you gave
you have broken your word to me   do not do so
why make promises   protesting your innocence
when all your vows are simply a defence
where are the assurances you gave your slave
you break your promises your word   do not do so

O you whose court lies beyond   being and non-being
you transgress the bounds of being   do not so

112

When the face of the Beloved appeared to Mansur
at the moment of union
it was right that the gallows should carry him all the way
to the origin

I tore off a strip of his gown   the length of a turban
it consumed me from head to foot   with my reason

113

If a tree could move and displace itself
either by foot or by wing
it would not suffer the agony of the saw
or the sharp blows of the axe

and if the sun did not travel
each night on foot or by wing
how would the world be lit again at dawn
if salt water did not rise from the sea into the sky
how would the garden get its life-giving rain
and when the raindrop leaves its place in its ground
returning to the ocean
it finds a shell and there becomes a pearl

did not Joseph leave his father   weeping
but at the end of his travels
arrive at victory and sovereignty and joy
did not Mohammed travel to Medina
and become lord and king of a hundred lands

even if you are footless   make that inner journey
like rubies absorbing the imprint of the sunbeam

travel from your self into yourself
for on the way
the earth will become a gold-mine under your feet
let the acrimony or bitterness in you turn sweet
just as briny ground will still yield
a thousand varieties of fruit

seek sweetness from that sun
Shams pride of Tabriz
for every plant and tree gains lustre from it

114

Stealthily like a thief   your spirit enters my soul
O graceful cypress of mine   splendour of my garden
when you go do not go without me   O soul of my soul do not go
without this body
O do not leave my sight   O flaming torch of mine

I tear open the seven heavens   go beyond the seven seas
when lovingly you gaze   into my errant soul
since you entered in my breast   I dispose of faith disbelief
O you whose sight is my faith   whose countenance my belief
you have left me headless and footless   sleepless   deprived
  of food
O come to me merry and laughing   O my Joseph of Canaan
through your grace I have become like a soul   and veiled thus
  from myself
O you whose being is hidden   in this hidden being of mine

115

God opens doors

116

Are you well   say   O my beloved
how do you fare in these ungentle times
night and day you are in my thoughts
how is it in these bloodthirsty times
with this fire that has fallen upon the world
with the smoke of the Mongol armies
in this sea and darkness and these hundred waves
how fares your heavy-laden ship

117

Go go my aerial soul on that strange journey
to the sea of meanings
for you are a rare pearl

you have passed through many stations if you remember
do not object to leaving this staging-post too
wash your wings of this mud and clay
and become light once again
why are you not flying after those friends
who have already flown

O break the pitcher and empty the water of life
into the stream
how long will you make the pitchers for others to break

from this mountain top let yourself plunge like a torrent
down to the sea
for these steep slopes offer no security
no foothold for the body

enough
do not distance yourself from the sun of Shams

to the east or the west
for through him you are the crescent moon

now at the full

118

O my love why do you linger
so long abroad
return from this exile
how long will you wander distraught
from one place to another

I have sent you a hundred letters
told you a hundred ways home
either you do not read the letters
or cannot find the way
if you do not read letters yet they read you
if you do not know the way you are in the hands
of he who does

return for in this earthly prison
nobody knows your worth
do not sit down with the stony-hearted
for you are a precious stone

you that have eluded heart and soul
washed your hands of heart and soul
you that have escaped the snares of the world
come back O falcon that returns

you are water and a stream   the one that people seek
you are lion and gazelle   and better than either one
how far is it from you to the soul   who are rarer than the soul
either you are mingled with the soul   or the rays of the loved one

you are moonlight at midnight   sugar on the lip
O my lord who are you really   what kind of marvel

beauty and splendour come from you
we bring our hearts and minds
this is the best of trades   the way you give and take
our lives are taken away   by this love of yours
so that we dissolve and die   like sugar on the tongue
but the very source of life   is to eat poison from your hand

119

We give thanks to that nothingness
which swept our lives away
through love of non-being   our souls have come to be

120

Strange
where has that beautiful heart-stealer gone
strange
where has that graceful cypress gone
like a candle he brought light into our midst
where has he gone without us   where has he gone

during the day my heart trembles like a leaf
at where alone at night he may have gone
go out on the road and ask of the wayfarers
where that fellow-traveller might have gone

go into the garden and ask the gardener
where the stem of that lovely flower has gone
go up on the roof and ask the watchman
where that peerless king may have gone

like a madman I wander in the desert
searching for where that gazelle has gone
I have wept so much that my eyes are like two rivers
where in those waters might that pearl have gone

and all night I ask of the moon and Venus
where in those heavens could my moon have gone
since he belongs with us how could he stay with others
since he is no longer here where has he gone

since his heart and soul are at one with God
if he has left this earthly world where has he gone
tell me plainly where Shams can be found
since it is he who said   the sun is not hidden

121

What is it bears witness to the existence of another world
changes of state   the disappearance of things past
the new day the new evening the new garden the new snare
at every breath a new thought   new riches new joy

where do these new things come from   and where do the old
ones go
if not beyond our sight   into an infinite world
like the water of a stream   which seems always the same
but renews itself constantly   so where does that come from

122

If the world of my life stopped turning
it would be turned by he who makes the heavens turn
if this army of mine were destroyed by the evil eye
at the word of my king armies would come down from the sky
if my garden was laid waste by the winter winds
my sovereign spring would restore it once again
and if the tyrant Pharaoh enslaved
just a few of its leaves
the hand of Moses would lead them home one by one

123

He is my soul   do not touch him
he is everything to me   do not cut him off
he is my bread   he is my water
nothing compares to his garden of hope
he is arbour and bower   he is flowing stream
red of apple   green of willow tree
he is constant   he is temperate
light of my heart   bring him back to me

124

O people   members of humanity
do not expect to find
anything human in me

even a madman could not conceive
what I have in my heart
his star has been eclipsed
fleeing from my passion

for I have mixed with death   and flown to not being

125

Our death is a wedding with eternity
what is the hidden meaning of this
God is One

the rays of the sun are divided
as they stream through the windows
close the shutters and that division goes
and the multiplicity of the bunch of grapes
is fused in the juice that flows from them

everyone who lives by the light of God
benefits from the death of their earthly form
do not speak good or ill of them
for they have passed beyond good and evil

fix your gaze on what is real and true
and do not try to speak of what cannot be seen
so that he may implant an eye within your eye
which is the eye of the eye and from which escapes
nothing mysterious or hidden

but when the gaze is turned towards the light of God
under such a light what could remain unseen

126

When I am asleep and mouldering in the grave
if you come to visit me I shall emerge forthwith
for me you are like the blast of the trumpet
rallying the dead on judgment day
so what else could I do

dead or alive wherever you are I am too
without your breath I am a lifeless silent flute
but what airs I play when you breathe into my reed
this miserable instrument of yours
has become reliant on your sugar lips
think to this wretch for he is seeking you

if I do not happen upon your moonlike face
I shall cover my head in mourning
if I do not find your sweet lips   I shall bite my own hands

127

O my friend   do not leave me friendless
do not leave me   do not abandon me
the soul of your servant comes to ask
for clemency
do not leave me alone without mercy

you are a doctor   more than that
you are the Jesus of our time   do not leave me sick
you said   you are my companion in the cave
do not leave me like this   alone in the cave

in your eyes   one night's absence is nothing
but it is me you should ask whether it is a lot or a little
do not abandon me
do not extinguish in my breast even this small flame
a tiny flame is still something   do not leave me

I have no breath left   even so
pay heed to me once more
do not leave me   do not abandon me now

128

Die die in this love die
for when you die through this love
you will receive the life of the spirit

die die and do not fear death
for you will leave this earth
and get to heaven

die die and cut yourself off
from the flesh of this world
for the carnal is a bond and you its prisoner

get hold of an axe and break out of that jail
for when you do
you will all be kings princes

die die before the king of beauty
for when you do you will be potentates

die die and come out
from behind that cloud
like a radiant full moon

be silent   be silent now
for silence is the breath of that death
but you are in thrall to life
and will not embrace silence

129

Do not despair   my soul   for hope is here
the hope of every soul has come
from the unseen
do not despair if Mary is no longer there for you
for that light which drew Jesus to heaven has appeared

do not despair   my soul
in the darkness of this prison
for the king who freed Joseph has arrived
Jacob has come out from behind the curtain
and Joseph who tore open Zuleikha's veil has come

O you who have spent the night crying Lord   Lord
he who heard the call   my Lord   has come
O you who have suffered pain so long
be happy now   for a remedy has come
O you whose cell was locked
open it now   for here is the key to it
O you who fasted even at that high table
break your fast now   for the new moon has come

be silent be silent now   for with the command
Be
the shock of wonder surpasses   anything you can say

130

That placeless place

131

Last night I renewed my vow
I swore an oath by your soul
that I would not take my eyes off your face
that even if you struck me with your blade
I would not turn away

that I would seek no succour from another
since in separation from you lies my pain
and if l let out a cry
when you cast me into the fire
I would not be a real man

I rose from your path like dust
and to dust will return again

132

Go lay your head on your pillow and leave me alone
to wander   broken   through the night
I and the waves of melancholy   alone from dark until morning

come if you will and be merciful
or be cruel and go
or stay away from me in case you too
should fall into calamity
choose the path of well-being not misfortune

I and my flowing tears have crept into the corner of grief
these tears of mine will turn the water-mill
a hundred times over

133

You have taken the decision to leave   like sweet life itself
remember
you have saddled the horse of separation
remember

you will find true friends on earth and in heaven
but you made a promise to your erstwhile friend   remember

I did things which angered you
O friend without spite   remember the nights with me
and each night when you lay down that moonlike face
on your pillow
remember the time when you laid your head on my knees

like Farhad I breathe the thin air
of the mountains of separation from you
O you for whom Khosrow and the beautiful Shirin
were no more than slaves

on the shore of the sea of my eyes
you looked out over the plain of love
full of pale flowers and sprigs of saffron

my burning sighs rise up to the heavens
remember how Gabriel from the highest point cried out
O Lord   amen

O Shams-e Tabriz from the day I first saw your face
love of your countenance has become my faith
O you whose very being manifests
the glory of religion

remember

134

(That encounter that meeting)

135

O morning breeze come tell me about the cheeks the mole
of Shams-uddin
carry from China to Constantinople
the musk and amber of Khotan

if you have a greeting from those sweet lips
tell me
and if you have a message from that hard heart
bring it to me

what worth has my head
that I should offer to sacrifice it for him
say to me again   the name of Shams-uddin
that I may lay down my soul at his feet
he has clothed me in a robe of honour
and fine garments
his beauty is my shirt   his love my gown
his scent fills my nostrils
his cup has made me drunk
O cup-bearer take heed   bring no more wine

Shams-uddin perfumes my senses
what need have I of incense or ambergris
or the musk of Tartary

Shams-uddin resides in my heart Shams-uddin ennobles my soul
Shams-uddin my only pearl Shams-uddin my ready gold
it is not I alone who sing Shams-uddin Shams-uddin
the nightingale in the garden and the partridge on the mountain-side
repeat his name

with the beauty of the heavenly maidens and the gardens of
  paradise
Shams-uddin is the perfect man the glory of the great
Shams-uddin is the bright day the heavens circling at night
he is the precious stone hidden in the depths of the ground

Shams-uddin is Jamshid's cup Shams-uddin the mighty ocean
possessed of the breath of Jesus and Joseph's countenance

with all my soul I pray God
to give me secret happiness with him
may our souls be joined together again
and Shams-uddin be by my side

136

Look   look
how autumn has come upon the garden
the heart-rending signs on leaf and branch
the trees sighing on all sides
in their hundreds

moist eyes and parched lips
are never without cause
nor the pallor of a broken heart

sorrow's raven has entered the bower
marching up and down
and asking arrogantly
where are the flowers then

where are the lily and the dog-rose
the tulip and the jasmine
where is the green-clothed lawn
and the purple Judas-tree
where are the tender fruits
and the bees' honeycomb
every milk-giving breast is dry

where is the sweet-voiced nightingale
and the ringdove
the peacock fine as an idol
and the parrots where have they gone

137

Finally you have flown off   and gone to that hidden place
strange   it is strange
which road did you take from this world
you beat your wings and feathers   breaking out of your cage
you took off and departed   towards the realms of the spirit

you were like a prize falcon   in the clutches of an old woman
when you heard the falcon's drum you flew to that other domain
you were a rapturous nightingale   living among owls
when the scent of the flowers reached you
you flew to the rose garden

you suffered many a hangover from drinking this sour wine
in the end you took your leave   to go to the eternal tavern
like an arrow you flew directly to the target of happiness
flying there straight and true   from the bow here

this world like a false ghoul offered you many a sign
but you ignored all those   and went to that world that has none

138

I have grown old through grief for him
but when you say the name Tabriz
all my youth comes back again

139

These caravans which one after another
set off on the next stage
how is it that you do not turn your head
towards them
how is it that your heart
does not throb with desire
does it not hear   from front and rear
the cries of the camel-drivers
the peal of the camel-bells

140

It is not I who speak these words   love speaks them

141

At the time of the evening prayer
when the sun sets
the way of the senses closes
and the way of the invisible opens up
then the angel of sleep leads men's souls to the threshold
like a shepherd watching over his flock

in that land beyond   those plains of the spirit
what strange cities what heavenly gardens he shows them
the spirit perceives
a thousand marvellous forms and faces
when sleep erases from it the imprint of this world

it is as if
the soul had always resided in that country
for it no longer remembers this earth and its travails
and from all the material things for which it trembled
it has become so distant
it no longer feels the bite or sting of grief

142

(That presence)

143

Anyone to whom the mystery of love
has been revealed
is no more
because he has effaced himself in love

place a burning candle in front of the sun
and see how its brightness is subsumed in those rays
the candle no longer exists   but is transmuted into light
there is no sign of it   yet it has become
a sign itself
the same is true of the fire of the body
in the glow of the spirit
it does not remain a fire but becomes that light

the stream flows down
searching for the sea
losing itself when it drowns in it

as long as the search goes on   its end is unknown
but when it is found   the search becomes redundant

144

The source of all my thoughts
the images I have in my head

is your breath alone
as if I were nothing but

had no existence beyond
your discourse   your words

145

How could I know that this dark passion
would drive me mad
turn my heart into a hell   my eyes into raging torrents
like the river Jaihūn
how could I know that this flood
would carry me away suddenly
and toss me about like a ship
on a Red Sea of blood
the waves breaking up that ship   plank by plank
sucking them down one by one
into a whirlpool

that a monster would rear its head   gulping the water
and that such a boundless sea would suddenly
turn into a desert   a waterless plain
which a great devouring serpent would split in two
and cast me down like Korah into a pit
in its anger

and when these metamorphoses occurred
leaving neither desert nor sea
how could I know how it came about
since the how was drowned in the how-less

and how could I know about so many things
that I did not know
since my mouth was full of water
and a dose of opiates

146

For forty years wisdom oppressed my mind
now at the age of sixty-two
I am on the run from prudence

147

O you of whose beauty the world is only a sign
your beauty is the end   everything else is secondary
if the painter did not have your loveliness
as a subject
what would be the point of his paintings   his murals

a hundred thousand candles live in the expectation
of being a flame in the furnace of your affection
your exquisite curls are the necklace around my throat
in these ringlets   my love   the bird of the spirit has nested

you ask when you will enter the court of that king
but the one has no boundary and the other no core
who has granted all this to us   if not Shams-uddin
with that power which turns a seed into a tree

148

Don't you understand what the rebeck is saying
about being filled with tears   gutted
I am like skin that has been stripped from the flesh
how could I not suffer terrible pain at this

and the piece of wood says also
I was once a green branch   tall as a rider
but it snapped beneath me and left me without a stirrup

O kings   we are all in exile
listen to my words   *to God is the returning*
we have come from God into this world
and after this circuit we shall go back to him
our cries are like the bells of the caravan
or thunder when the clouds gather

O traveller   do not give your heart to this sojourn
for you will suffer when it is torn away
you have already passed through many stages
from sperm to young man
do not commit yourself to them
so that when the time comes you may move on

if you distance yourself from this world
you will in time receive your recompense

believe in him who has believed in you
hold firm
for he is both the beginning and the end

find him

149

At the time of the evening prayer   when people set out meals and lights
I with the image of my beloved   am weeping my heart out
my tears serving as ablutions   my devotions catching fire
setting my mosque ablaze   when I hear the call to prayer

I have lost my sense of direction   so now my prayers have lapsed
though you and I are always tested by lapses
strange indeed the prayer   of he who is out of his mind
tell me   is it right
for he knows nothing of time   nor anything of the world
which position is this   is it the eighth one
and which verse am I reading   since I do not possess a tongue

how shall I beat on the door of truth   neither hand nor heart remain
since you carried them off   may God in heaven save me
but I have heard nothing from God   since I missed my prayers
if my genuflexions are complete   or someone has become an imam

150

Whoever does not have in him
that tint   that hue of love
in the eyes of God is only wood or stone

151

He who made me drunk without wine   where is he
he who separated me
from my heart and soul   where is he
he who diverted me from my vows   my penitence
where is he
he for whom men's souls cry out at dawn   where is he
he for the loss of whom   we are laid low
where is he

he is the soul of the soul   spirit of the spirit
if he cannot be contained in one place   what of it

152

On the day of my death   when my bier goes by
do not imagine I am pining for this world
do not weep for me and cry alas   for then
you will truly fall into the devil's snare

when you see my cortege do not cry dolefully
for that time will be for me one of communion
and if you commit me to the grave do not say farewell
for the grave only hides the gathering of souls

after the descent think to the rising
how could their going down
affect the sun or moon
to you it seems like setting but it is actually rising

though the tomb seems a prison it sets free the soul
what seed goes into the earth that does not burgeon
why then should you doubt the seed of man

what pitcher is lowered that does not come up full
so why should this Joseph complain about the well
when your mouth closes here it will open there
and your song of triumph will be in the placeless air

153

If the holy spirit were to unveil itself
the mind and soul would seem as real as flesh

154

(That being)

155

O send a wave out of nothingness
to sweep me away
how long must I pace nervously
the shores of the sea

156

Of the book of my life only one page remains
my soul is impatient for that deliverance
in that book is written a word sweeter than sweetness
and even the moon is upset at its beauty

eternal life shines down on the garden leaves
no fevered imaginings   no fear of demise
his name was the leaf of a book in which was displayed
the kingdom of God
and the secrets of all those who are pure
lay bathed in the twilight there

on the folds of that page the light of God was revealed
Shams-al-haq of Tabriz   bright pupil of the eye

157

All things are indivisible
the world's harp has a single string

158

O lovers lovers
it is time to forsake this world
the drum of departure from heaven
reaches the ear of the soul
the camel-driver is about already lining up the camels
and asking our pardon
O travellers why do you slumber still

these sounds in front and behind
are those of the camel-bells the hubbub of departure
every minute a life and soul set off
into the surrounding emptiness the void

from these upturned candles of stars
this deep blue awning of heaven
a wondrous host has come down
so that the mystery might be made clear

with the circling of the spheres
a deep sleep came over you
alas for this trivial life beware this heavy sleep

O heart seek out the beloved O friend search for the Friend
O watchman stay awake the watchman should not sleep

159

I have prayed so much that my life has become a prayer
to the point where
when people see my face they turn to pray

160

If wheat should grow from my grave
the bread they make would make people tipsy
the baker and the dough would both go crazy
and the oven itself sing drunken ditties

if you make a pilgrimage to my tomb
my headstone will be dancing in your sight
O brother come not without your tambourine
for at God's banquet sorrow is not right
with the chin bound up and quiet in the grave
while the mouth chews opium and sugar plum
a gift from the beloved

tear a strip off my shroud and tie it to your breast
and your soul will find the door to the hidden tavern
where on every side you will hear
the din the hubbub of voices
and the sound of the harp
for everything that is done gives birth to something else

God created me out of the wine of love
and I remain a lover

even though death should pulverise me
and turn me to dust

I am the essence of drunkenness itself
in the wine of love lie my beginnings
tell me what drinking leads to if not this

my soul will fly without pausing
to the towering spirit of Shams-uddin of Tabriz

NOTES

These translations have had a long gestation. In 1976 I was awarded an Arts Council writer's bursary and decided to spend the year not only on my own poetry but also on translation, partly to provide a less personal, more technical challenge. I had first come across Rumi's work during my three years in Isfahan from 1964-67 and was also inspired by Nicholson's translations. The poet and scholar Shafi'i-Kadkani had kindly given me a copy of his selected edition, which contains 466 ghazals (sometimes abridged) and I worked through this, referring to some other materials as well. However, by the end I was not satisfied with what I had done and filed all my work away. I felt I had simply not got hold of Rumi.

During the subsequent decades two things happened. First, Rumi became widely known and very popular, and secondly I published a book of translations of Hafez' ghazals. After that I decided to look back at my Rumi files to see if I could do anything with them and after some hesitation resumed my work. I initially used the Darvīsh collected edition which I had to hand but since this contains some poems which may not be authentic and is unsatisfactory in other ways I obtained the complete text edited by Forūzānfar which is generally reckoned to be the most reliable. However, since the Darvish edition was very widely distributed, I have given the numbers for both editions below (F for Foruzanfar, D1 and D2 for Darvish: the latter is in two volumes). Where relevant I have also given the Nicholson Latin number.

While Foruzanfar's edition represents a massive work of scholarship, we need to be cautious about assuming that it is definitive. Whereas with most other Persian poets the text comes directly from the author, Rumi's ghazals were apparently written down by his students and followers as or after they heard the Master declaim them and were later checked by him. Even if this process was highly organized it is quite possible that some texts went astray or were not gathered together with the others. For example, the Chester Beatty manuscript which Nicholson used is not entirely consistent with Foruzanfar's edition, and there is an entire Turkish edition dating from around the same time. It is thus possible that further research will turn up more materials, or reconcile existing variants. Further research may also help establish a chronology of the ghazals (see Lewis in Lewisohn, 2014).

Since this is a book of poetry rather than an academic text I have tried to keep things as simple as possible without sacrificing its integrity. The selection and order of poems is my own. In many cases I have translated part of a ghazal, and this is indicated by the line references. The Persian line is long by English standards, often coming to about 14 syllables, and typically divided into two halves.

For the language, I have used the words Persian and Farsi interchangeably. Both derive from the name of a southern province which was its source; p and f are close in the language. The ancient and modern name of the country is Iran and its people refer to themselves as Iranians.

As regards transcription I have done just enough for general readers to get some sense of the sound and Persian-speakers to recognize the original. I have indicated long vowels with a horizontal accent and followed the usual convention of transcribing *qaf* as q and *ghain* as gh. The word *va* meaning 'and' is usually pronounced 'o' in poetry. There are no capital letters in Farsi so I have used them sparingly in the English where appropriate. I have indicated long vowels the first time a name is used but omitted them thereafter.

Quotations from the Koran are in italics in both the text and notes, giving the chapter and verse numbers. I have used the transcription of the name of the Prophet Mohammed in the form given in Haïm's dictionary. My three interpolations near the end of the text are in parentheses.

I have kept my notes on the poems to the minimum necessary to make sense of them or the references within them. However, in some cases I have briefly addressed issues related to their content or my translation of them. Some other translations are listed in the bibliography and readers may wish to refer to them for comparison. It is, after all, an imperfect, indeed partial, art.

1 F1. D1–1. Lines 1–4. This is the first poem in Foruzanfar's edition, which suggests that it is about the initial encounter between Rumi and Shams. There are two issues in the very first line *ei rastakhīz-e nagahān vei rahmat bi muntahā*. *Rastakhīz* means the day of resurrection and Rumi seems to be comparing his meeting with Shams with the greatest of all events at the end of the world. However *khīz* is a potent word in Farsi and I wonder if here it has a more general sense of rising up or apparition. In the end I decided to stay with resurrection, although it does have the connotation of Christ's resurrection which is inapposite here. Secondly, although *rahmat* is usually translated as 'mercy', the latter is used in two different ways in English, one as the mitigation of punishment (to show mercy) and the other in the broad religious sense of 'loving mercy', which is the meaning here. I have tried to capture this by expanding the line. See also the similar note on *rahmat* in Fouchécour, 2017: 120n2.

2 F2730. D2–1365. At the end I have translated the Arabic phrase *lā makān* as 'placeless place'.

3 F310. D1–310. N VII. The suffix *-uddīn* means '-of religion'. The Nicholson version has an additional couplet reading 'Love's fingers tear up, root and stem/every house where sunbeams fall from love' after line 8.

4 F633. D1–637. Lines 1–5. The first line involves a play on Shams' name, which means sun in Arabic. The moon is a symbol of beauty.

5 F5. D1–2. Lines 1–5.

6 F7. D1–7. Lines 1–8. *Hal ata.* The first two words of sura/chapter 76 of the Koran. Khalidi translates as 'surely there came …'

7 F2080. D2–714. Line 9.

8 F362. D1–362.

9 F163. D1–165. In line 2, if one translated *bahānehāye* as 'excuses' rather than 'pretexts' the half-line might refer to Shams, but that would run over from the previous couplet, which is unusual. In the last line the reference is to *aqīq* (agate) for which Yemen was famous.

10 F1220. D1–1226. I have translated this fast-paced poem a little more freely, but retained the reference to the liver which in Farsi has emotional connotations, as in the expression *jegaram kabāb shod* – my liver has been turned into kebab. I have translated this in a later poem as 'gutted'.

11 F117. D1–119. Lines 1–9. The Chinese had a reputation for beauty in Persian poetry. 'Shaking his sleeve' is a sign of munificence.

12 F14. D1–15. Lines 8–11. The word *fanā*, which I translate by 'annihilation' is an important Sufi term denoting the entire destruction of the self.

13 F2152. D2–787. Line 11. Along with repetitive chanting, music and dancing, hand-clapping was often part of Sufi rituals intended to transport participants out of themselves.

14 F2214. D2–849. NXXXVIII. Among other differences, Nicholson omits the final couplet. 'The moon' presumably refers to Shams himself. Iraq refers not to the modern country but, like Khorasan, to a province of Iran. This is one of the many poems which celebrate the co-presence of Rumi and Shams. The latter also sees their meeting and companionship as destiny (Chittick, 2004: 186).

15 F1826. D2–460. Lines 1–5. The *houris* were the beautiful beings, sometimes described as maidens, who awaited the faithful as a reward in paradise.

16 F2788. D2–1423. Line 9. The text refers to *tanāqaz*, contradictions.

17 F1377. D2–8. The Ka'aba is the shrine at the centre of Mecca around which pilgrims circle.

18 F722. D1–726.

19 F21. D1–21. Lines 1–4. Steingass' dictionary gives *shokr e ne'mat* as 'acknowledgement of benefits or favours received'. I have paraphrased. The Koranic quotation is from chapter 14, verse 32.

20 F639. D1–643. In Persian poetry Turks were regarded as symbols of both beauty and cruelty. Arabs were viewed as more neighbourly, though not altogether favourably.

21 F1909. D2–543. Lines 4–5.

22 F622. D1–626. Here, the appellation *al-haq* is a religious one and could be translated as 'the true' or even 'the godly' although in a social context, referring to a king or leader, might be read as 'the just'. I have avoided adding a second 'q' to *haq* since I think it adds nothing phonemically to the English.

23 F181. D1–183.

24 F2003. D2–637. This rich poem draws together the natural, the human and the divine in a complex array. However, several lines remain problematic. I have translated *chaman* here as 'grounds'. It is always a difficult term, but Rumi does not use the usual word for garden here. I have translated *zīr-e lagan*, literally beneath the screen, as 'behind this' assuming that the screen is that of appearances and the lamp/light the reality behind. The reference to Mary is to the immaculate conception and the hope of children. I assume the 'children of the garden' refers to the trees and bushes.

25 F69. D1–69.

26 F84. D1–86. The refrain is the word *tanhā*, 'alone'.

27 F393. D1–393.

28 F332. D1–332. NXVI. Lines 1–6. The stone building of the Ka'aba is the focus of the pilgrimage to Mecca. It dates from pre-Islamic times and when Mohammed took control of it he emptied it of all the pagan idols inside. The Magian temple refers to the pre-Islamic Zoroastrian religion of Iran, cf. the Magi in the Christian story.

29 F2971. D2–1606. Line 3.

30 F2010. D2–644. Khezr (Arabic Khidr) appears in the Koran (18:61–83) as a mystical guide to Moses but also figures in Iranian mythology in other ways. He is associated with the water of life and was believed to have frustrated Alexander the Great (an Iranian bogeyman) in his search for it. *Knowledge from Us* is a quotation from the Koran 18:65 and *lam yakon* is at the beginning of sura/chapter 98, The Manifest Proof (not sura 140, which does not exist, as stated in Arberry 2009: 418).

31 F251. D1–251. One of the fullest expositions of Rumi's chain of being. The question and answer refer to the primordial pact established in the Koran at 7:172. The reference to the creation of the sky is also to the Koran 41:11.

32 F3. D1–4. Lines 1–5. The opening of a long ghazal, which has been translated in its entirety by Arberry as the first one in his book. This kind of antithetical pattern is one of Rumi's poetic devices. In this case, as in many others, the verse pursues the aural logic of sounds, e.g. *chandān keshesh* ... *chandān cheshesh* ... While the first three lines could be from a European courtly love poem, the remainder make clear the underlying spiritual purpose.

33 F1453. D2–84. Last line omitted.

34 F1957. D2–591.

35 F1759. D2–390. Line 5. For a complete translation of this ghazal see Lewis, 2008:159–60.

36 F940. D1–944. Lines 1–6. This is one of the ghazals which explores the theme of being and nothingness. It is difficult to find the right English word to translate the final verb *afzūd*, which has the sense of augmenting, enhancing or nurturing.

37 F1397. D2–28. Lines 1–6. In the first line *ei ajbā* could also be translated as 'O wonder'. There are several variants and possible translations of the word I have translated as 'confounded', one of which could be 'pounded' as in a pestle.

38 F648. D1–652. Rumi here controversially questions the necessity of making the pilgrimage to Mecca which is one of the basic requirements of Islam, if it is possible.

39 F110. D1–112. A phrase such as 'the reflection of the reflection' exemplifies Rumi's drive towards essence or origin. There is a typically neat word play on the latter: *asl* means origin/root and *aslan* 'at all'.

40 F38. D1–38. Lines 1–4. I have found my final lines difficult to translate because there is not a simple equivalence between the various terms for cognition (knowledge, wisdom, learning, mind, brain) in the two languages. This is hardly surprising given the distance in time and place. However, the general message seems clear: the mind can be as much an obstacle to spiritual insight as an aid. This should be seen in the context of the long-term debate within Islamic theology between reason and revelation (see Text and Context).

41 F1047. D1–1052. We do not know whom this tender, physical poem was about but it seems to have been an adolescent boy or young man, always remembering that the third person singular pronoun 'oo' could be male or female.

42 F111. D1–113. Lines 1–4. A glimpse perhaps of the hostility and insinuations that Rumi's relationship with Shams generated. The remaining three lines are more conventional but do mention suspicion, *gamān.*

43 F566. D1–570. NXXI. I am not quite sure about the physics of the rope-trick but the word *chenbar* means loop, hoop, circle or coil. Here I think it is the last, coiling oneself like a spring before jumping. Near the end, the word *zauq* which I have translated as 'ecstasy' literally means 'taste' but in Sufism has a powerful sense of extraordinary, inexpressible, divine joy. The water of life could be capitalised: it has its full mystical meaning.

44 F221. D1–223. It is worth noting that the word for resurrection here is the usual one, *qiāmat*, not *rastakhīz* which occurs in No 1. The reference to children or young people arising with white hair is from the Koran 73:17.

45 F299. D1–299. For the reference to Khezr see No 30. 'Not out of spite but goodwill': this is the best I can make of *nei ze kīn bal ze ehtesāb*, but it is stretching the last word. The allusion to tale-telling, *ghamāz*, is usually pejorative; here the sense is of a willing disclosure of the mysteries of nature.

46 F211. D1–213. Lines 1–8. Rumi inherited a long tradition of seasonal poems, going back to Rudaki (see Text and Context) and this is just one example from the *Divan*. Spring had and still has an added significance as the beginning of the Persian new year, at the equinox. In line 4 of the original *sanbalē* means an ear of corn but I think the context here suggests *sanbal*, hyacinth. In line 6, Darvīsh annotates *sarē* as good or pure and I have followed this.

47 F2602. D2–1337. Line 7.

48 F291. D1–291. The theme of night as a valuable time for prayer and spiritual meditation occurs in a number of ghazals. The italicised reference is to Koran 92:1. Near the end I have translated *sāheb nazari* as 'insight into what is'. It is an important Sufi phrase referring to those who possess true mystical vision.

49 F1000. D1–1004.

50 F231. D1–233. The italicised reference is to the Koran 22:6. Although *sahrā* can mean desert (cf sahara) the word corresponding to our 'desert' is *biābān*, a place without water. Here *sahrā* refers to open, arable land where plants and even crops may grow.

51 F809. D1–813. Lines 1–8. The last line gives the key to the parable.

52 F1708. D2–339. Final line. The regressive formula (soul of the soul of ...) is used many times in the *Divan*, pointing to the ultimate origin or source of things.

53 F731. D1–735. Lines 1–5. This is one of the many poems in the *Divan* that refer to the Sufi martyr Mansūr al-Hallaj and his famous/infamous statement (see Text and Context). It has a clever texture of words that are aurally quite similar but semantically different.

54 F1201. D1–1207. Lines 1–4. Carnelian or cornelian is a translucent brownish-red precious stone. I have translated *nāz* here as 'charm'. Although it has several meanings this seems to me the right one for this delicately erotic poem, and the word is still widely used today.

55 F114. D1–116. Final couplet.

56 F861. D1–865. N XXIII. *The morning splendour*: Koran 93:1. This line is problematic. A number of the final sections of the Koran begin with an evocation of day or night, adducing the beauty and majesty of creation, and this is one. However, Rumi's reference to this reads literally 'God did not describe his face as morning splendour except out of jealousy'. I have paraphrased the line in order to emphasize the paradox. I am still not sure about its real intention, and it does not follow on from the first half of the line, but Rumi took delight in such breath-taking paradoxes. Nicholson's version has two additional lines and other differences.

57 F1486. D2–112. Lines 1–2.

58 F768. D1–772. I have translated *makān-e lā makāni* as 'placeless place' although it could be rendered as 'worldless world'.

59 F1327. D1–1334. Lines 1–2. One of the few poems which refers to the events of the time. Even here however Rumi finds consolation in the common superstition that treasure could be found beneath ruins. The Mongols are referred to as *tatār*. The Discourses of Shams also quote the saying 'for I am with the broken' (Chittick, 2004:12; 358).

60 F765. D1–769. Lines 1–3.

61 F1295. D1–1301. Lines 1–7. One of many ghazals in the *Divan* in praise of the famous Mevlevi Sufi whirling dance; for references to others see Chittick, 1983: 325–29. The first line reads literally 'the soul of the soul of the soul …' In the Discourses of Shams the dance is evoked beautifully as appearing as light as a leaf floating on water but actually as weighty as a mountain (Chittick, 2004: 114). In my penultimate line ('stamp under your feet all that is not he/it') while the word *vei* usually means he or she I have come across a translation of it as 'it' and think that is consistent with the rest of the poem here. However it does affect the meaning of the poem and must remain open to question.

62 F783. D1–787. Lines 1–3.

63 F1393. D2–24. Lines 1–11. Some of the ghazals take the form of a dialogue. The result can be a bit formulaic as here but it is worth including it as an example of the genre. In the first line of the Persian Rumi uses the word *dowlat* twice. It can mean either government or power, like the French noun *pouvoir*.

64 F2351. D2–987. Lines 16–17. Shaker-bells are small bells attached to a staff and are used in English Morris dancing. I imagine something similar here. I have translated *do beyti* as rhyming couplet.

65 F652. D1–656. Lines 1–4. The word used is *bandē* meaning slave or servant but even in ordinary conversation this is still sometimes employed as a form of deference, and I have simply translated it here as 'man'.

66 F351. D1–351. Lines 1–3. The remainder of this poem continues in the same vein but with different images and I have judged that this short excerpt is more powerful on its own. Until we have a translation of the entire *Divan* – a massive task which has nevertheless been mooted—the issues of selection both of and within poems will remain.

67 F331. D1–331. Galen was a famous ancient Greek physician. The end of this poem addresses one of the key concerns of Muslim (and indeed Christian) theologians, namely the relationship between God's will and human free will.

68 F2530. D2–1165.

69 F947. D1–951. Another ghazal which invokes the night as a time of prayer and spirituality. *Arise in the night* is from Koran 73:2. There is also an echo of Koran 76:26 '*And glorify him through the long night*'. The line about cooking is obscure. Raw and cooked are often used in Persian poetry as metaphors for the difference between inexperience or innocence on the one hand and experience or sophistication on the other. I have paraphrased this in terms of 'yet to learn'.

70 F1739. D2–370. Lines 1–8. There are several ghazals in the *Divan* in praise of the Muslim practice of fasting during Ramadan (Ramazan in Farsi).

71 F425. D1–425. Given the complex nature of the word I have translated *haqiqat* as both 'reality' and 'truth'. Both could be capitalised.

72 F678. D1–682. Lines 1–5.

73 F1634. D2–265.

74 F2251. D2–886. Lines 1–6.

75 F2407. D2–1043. The refrain is the first part of the Muslim statement of faith. It rejects polytheism. The second part acknowledges Mohammed as Prophet. Likewise 'are you not' recalls the question put to his creatures by God at the beginning of creation: am I not your lord? To which they answer, assenting: yes (Koran 7:172). The frequency of Koranic references in the *Divan* indicate the extent to which Rumi was steeped in the holy text, a fact missing from some of the popularised translations or versions. Collyrium was used as an eye-salve.

76 F577. D1–581. Line 7.

77 F1078. D1–1083. The companions were those who took refuge with Mohammed in a cave early in his prophethood. See Koran 18:9.

78 F840. D1–844. Final line.

79 F381. D1–381. The Simorgh was a mythical bird which had magical powers. It lived on Mount Qāf and if its shadow fell on a man he would become king. In Sufism it was also associated with saints. And it was sometimes compared to the phoenix. We do not know the background to this troubled poem but the juxtaposition of conflict and fame and reproof (*jang o nang o nām*) may express both the adulation and criticism that Rumi received.

80 F782. D1–786. Lines 1–9. Here Rumi is squarely in the tradition of seasonal poems, personifying the plants and birds in a courtly fashion. However, there are also spiritual overtones: the word used for my 'performance' is *samā'*, the whirling Sufi dance, and spring is referred to as a resurrection, *qiāmat*.

81 F2172. D2–807. Lines 7–9. *And he is with you*: see Koran 57:4.

82 F1049. D1–1054. Lines 1–3.

83 F49. D1–48. In line 1 with *āftābi* (light or sunny) here as elsewhere Rumi is invoking the meaning of *shams* as sun. In the same line, as well as meaning to freeze, the verb *afsordan* can mean to be depressed and Rumi may be playing on this double sense. The final reference is to an old rhyme about camels. Unusually the Darvish number for this ghazal is lower than the Foruzanfar one.

84 F824. D1–828. Final three lines. The final line is from Koran 50:16: *We created man and know what his soul murmurs to him; but We are nearer to him than his jugular vein.* (trans. Khalidi). As noted in Text and Context

Sufis often quoted and still quote this as justification for the 'inner way'. Much of the writing about Rumi is by people who are committed to Sufism and this can slip into uncritical hagiography. I have tried, however, to give some sense of how his work appears not only to such followers but to Muslims who do not necessarily share these ideas and who may take a more circumspect stance. In this book we also get occasional and sometimes surprising, even disconcerting, glimpses of Rumi the man. That said, he is revered as a poet and a spiritual figure by the vast majority of Iranians, and now has a very wide global following.

85 F823. D1–827. Lines 1–5. The poem ends not with a reference to Shams but with praise for Saladin, the king, and its philosophical, reflective tone perhaps reflects this. Despite its title, by no means all the ghazals in the *Divan* relate to Shams. It is sometimes referred to simply as 'the great *divan*'.

86 F74. D1–74. Qārūn (Korah) was a fabled rich and miserly man who was swallowed up with his treasures (Koran 28:76–82). The refrain *shavi bā mā* (you will...like/with us) is very evident in this ghazal.

87 F395. D1–395.

88 F678. D1–682. Final line. The word *bīs* is unusual, but is clearly negative. The French translation of Vitray-Meyerovitch and Mokri (1973:212) has 'vile'.

89 F981. D1–985. Although Rumi compared writing poetry to washing tripe for his guests to eat (Thackston, 1994: 77) he does elsewhere admit that when he began to write he felt a strong urge to do so and that it was satisfying and effective (ibid: 208).

90 F2899. D2–1534.

91 F1771. D2–402.

92 F1163. D1–1168. A three-line explosion of anger which may come as a shock to those who adopt a hagiographical approach to Rumi. *az do se mādē*:

literally 'from two three she-animals', e.g. dogs, although the word can refer to female humans. Chittick however (1983:147) translates mādē as 'unmanly'. The line is thus obscure but the invective is clear. I have used the colloquial English term 'copper' to translate *pol-e siāh* (dark money) which means precisely that. And 'quack' happily translates 'large ducks' which has the same connotations. According to another source Rumi used the expression 'brother of a whore' when angry (Chittick, 2004: 345). As the *Maqālāt* shows Shams could be even more scabrous.

93 F473. D1–474.

94 F505. D1–506. Lines 1–7. The 'loveless heart' is a reminder of the importance of the heart, as against the mind, in Sufi teaching, as in the *hadith* '*Neither My heaven nor My earth embraces Me, but the heart of my believing servant does embrace me.*' (Chittick, 2004: 126; 127). The heart is a key theme in classical Persian poetry, especially that of Hafez. Unlike in western romantic poetry, where it is largely or purely emotional, the heart in Persian poetry is the source of its own kind of knowing, which rivals or even outdoes that of the mind.

95 F525. D1–529. Lines 1–4. According to a popular belief the sun sank into a well at sunset and came out again at dawn. In my final lines the text actually refers to a (handsome) Turk who has come back into his tent, but the word *khargāh* means both tent and halo.

96 N XII. Nicholson, who was using the manuscript in the Chester Beatty collection, included this poem but it is not in either Darvish or Foruzanfar. It may therefore not be by Rumi but as far as I know has not been firmly attributed to anyone else. Lewis (2000: 302) notes that in Arberry's opinion Foruzanfar might not have taken sufficient account of the Chester Beatty Ms., which is now in Dublin. Manuscript variants are a familiar problem with texts of this age. This is a fine poem so I decided on balance to include it, but with this cautionary note. Nicholson thought the opening lines reflected the influence of Platonism. Note the reference here again to the 'placeless place', *lā makān*. In line 3 of the original the word *noktē* ('utterance' or fine point) is typical of Rumi, and there are other examples of his characteristic vocabulary in the poem. The final lines contrast the Christian appeal to the Son of God and the Muslim appeal to the Oneness of God.

97 F1521. D2–151. N XXX. The sleeves of garments were typically loose and capacious.

98 F1553. D2–184. Final line.

99 F1553. D2–184. Lines 1–4. The roses might be concealed in the capacious sleeves (see 97). These lines echo the *hadith*: *congregation is a mercy* (Chittick, 2004:31).

100 F2342. D2–978

101 F493. D1–494. In the Koran it says that the prophet Idris asked the angel of death to take his soul temporarily and then return it to his body, which he did. Sometimes identified with Enoch or Hermes Trismegistus.

102 F1690. D2–321. N XXXII. Lines 1–7. Abu Lahab was the uncle of Mohammed who refused to support him and offer him protection. At first sight the line does not make sense until one realises that immolation by the beloved is such an honour that only the worst would not be granted it. For the curse on Abu Lahab see Koran 111:1.

103 F239. D1–240. N II. Lines 1–8. One of the best known ghazals through Nicholson's fine translation. I sometimes wonder if Iris Murdoch got the title of her novel *A Severed Head* from here.

104 F1590. D2–221. Lines 1–4. The English word 'mundane' is derived from the French *monde*, meaning world.

105 F182. D1–184. Line 5. The reference is to Mount Safa near Mecca.

106 F996. D1–1000. N XXII. A famous mystical poet in the previous generation who reputedly met Rumi when he was a boy and recognised his genius. He is referred to a number of times in *Fihi Ma Fihi*.

107 F1462. D2–93. N XXXIV

108 N XVII. Like No 96 this poem is in Nicholson but not Darvish or Foruzanfar and the same caveat applies. 'Two bow-lengths distance' is a quotation from the Koran 53:9. It is a powerful poem but must have scandalised the orthodox in its rejection of the usual symbols and locations of faith, and may have been excluded from the canon at some point because of this. It is worth noting that the main French translation by Vitray-Meyerovitch and Mokri (1973) includes both poems but places them in an appendix.

109 F120. D1–122. This is the refrain of this poem, *asl-e kh(v)īsh ā*, repeated nine times in the original. The word *asl* is normally translated as 'origin' but I have used a more poetic equivalent here. The formula 'the X of the X' occurs again and again in the *Divan*, in an attempt to describe the quintessence of things. The poem echoes the *hadith* 'Begin with yourself' (Thackston, 1994: 178). For a discussion of *nafs* (ego-self) see Darr (2014).

110 F649. D1–653. N XIX. It is difficult to translate some of these spiritual terms. Where I have translated *serr-e tajali-ye azal* by 'until the eternal mystery was revealed' Nicholson has the more elegant 'theophany'.

111 F2054. D2–688. N XXXVII. Lines 1–7. The word *bandē* may be translated as either servant or slave, both metaphorical here.

112 F1288. D1–1294. Lines 1–2. Another poem referring to the Sufi martyr Mansur al-Hallaj.

113 F1142. D1–1147. N XXVII. There are slight differences in the Chester Beatty text.

114 F1786. D2–420. Lines 1–6. In ancient cosmology the number seven was significant, and here relates to the seven planets.

115 This is a traditional religious saying which is included in a number of ghazals including F217, F250, F313, F1052/ D1–219, D1–250, D1–313 and D1–1052. See also the note on *goshāyesh* in the *Maqālāt*: 'that unexpected opening granted by God' (my trans.) (Fouchécour, 2017: 92 n4). This was also the original sense of *fath/fotūh*.

116 F2670. D2–1305. Lines 1–4. As before the word for Mongol is *tātār*. The smoke might be from their camp fires or more likely burning cities. The vessel is probably metaphorical.

117 F2873. D2–1509.

118 F2572. D2–1207. Another poem about absence. Shams left and came, or was brought, back at least once.

119 F950. D1–954. Line 1.

120 F677. D1–681. The last line refers to a traditional Arabic saying: *al-shams lā yakhfi*. The play is of course on Shams' name.

121 F462. D1–462. Lines 9–12.

122 F592. D1–596. Lines 1–4. The tyrant Pharoah was conventionally contrasted with the liberator Moses who led the Israelites out of captivity.

123 F1280. D1–1286. Lines 1–4.

124 F1372. D2–3. Lines 3–4.

125 F833. D1–837. Lines 1–8. *God is one*: Koran 112:1. I am tempted here as elsewhere to capitalise words such as 'real' but as noted elsewhere there are no capitals in Persian. I have however translated *haq* as 'real and true' to try to capture more of the scope of this key term.

126 F1641. D2–272.

127 F1041. D1–1046. The reference to the cave is to Mohammed and his companion Abu Bakr hiding together in one during the flight from Mecca. In line 6 of the original the verb *miandāz* seems an odd word to use but I take the sense to be throwing out or away the fire. However, it could also be read as meaning 'do not leave me with this fire even if it is small, return and extinguish it'. This poem has the insistent refrain *magzār*, do not leave.

128 F636. D1–640. This ghazal reflects the *hadith* 'Die before you die' (Thackston, 1994: 14). Kadkani (No 113) glosses the last verb in the poem *nafīrīd* as *rugardān*, to turn ones face away. I have expressed this negatively as 'will not embrace'.

129 F631. D1–635. For the divine command 'Be' see the story of Mary in the Koran: '*When He decrees a matter, He merely says to it: "Be!" and it is'*. (3:45ff).

130 This is my translation of the Arabic term *lā makān* which Rumi and others used to express a mystical state, *lā* being the Arabic negative. See *inter alia* Nos 2, 58, 96 and 152.

131 F1559. D1–190.

132 F2039. D2–673. Lines 1–4. Foruzanfar has a long note on this poem which some believe was composed on Rumi's death-bed. The rest of the poem is powerful but disjointed: for a full translation see Arberry no 253 or Lewis 2008:56. Whereas I have translated *soudā* as melancholy here, Arberry has 'passion' and Lewis 'grief'.

133 F1063. D1–1065. The poem is strung together by the refrain *yād dār* (remember). Shirin is pronounced with two long 'i's. I have translated *sāf* by 'true' although the dictionary meaning is 'pure'. It is noteworthy that this poem, like many others, combines both Islamic and traditional Persian references, drawing on both strands in the culture.

134 The first of three headings I have interpolated (in parentheses) towards the end of the text in order to help draw the threads together, referring back here to No 1. From the initial encounter with Shams onwards, the notion of meeting pervades the *Divan*, carrying with it the mystical sense of meeting the Beloved or God. The word *vasl*, meaning union, is also important cf. the opening line of the poem on Hafez' tomb: *where are the good tidings of union*. Appropriately the old English verb to meet also has powerful resonances, including that of meeting one's maker. See also the section on 'Our Encounter' in the Discourses of Shams (Chittick, 2004: 179ff). One wonders whether the arrival of Shams might not have coincided with some feelings on Rumi's side, perhaps of staleness or a kind of spiritual impasse, which would have made him more receptive to his message. However, I know of no evidence of this.

135 F1081. D1–1086. Lines 1–12. Khotan was a region of western China famed for its beauty. Jamshid was a mythical Persian hero who possessed a magical cup in which he could see the whole world. It was believed that Jesus' breath could bring the dead to life. Like other Muslims Rumi revered Jesus as a prophet but did not believe he was the Son of God. He is mentioned quite frequently in the *Divan*, as is Mary. This paean of praise continues for several more lines but I think this is the best of it.

136 F1794. D2–429. Lines 1–7. Another example of the tradition of seasonal poems. The Persian relies heavily on repeated, rhythmic phrases which I could not make work in English. For a complete, literal translation of this long ghazal see Arberry No 223.

137 F3051. D2–1686. N XLVIII. Lines 1–7. Owls had, and still have, a negative reputation in Persian culture, as in Hedāyat's famous modern novel *The Blind Owl.*

138 F207. D1–209. N VI. Final line.

139 F17. D1–18. Lines 7–8.

140 F1520. D2–150. Line 15, first half.

141 F943. D1–947.

142 The second of my interpolations, drawing the text together. The presence of Shams, and being in his presence, is a central theme in the *Divan*, most sharply revealed by his absences. The theme ranges from the companionable happiness expressed in No 14 through to the much more intense interactions and relations expressed in many of the other poems. See also the section on 'Our Companionship' in the Discourses of Shams (Chittick, 2004: 211ff) and the touching statement on p.186: 'The goal of the existence of the world is for two friends to meet and look upon each other for the sake of God, far from caprice'.

143 F828. D832. Lines 1–6. The disappearances into something greater are presented in the Farsi as a series of paradoxes.

144 F1683. D2–314. Line 5. I have unpacked this dense, single line which is one of the strongest expressions of Rumi's debt to Shams.

145 F1855. D2–489. While *soudā* in the first line could be translated as melancholy that seems to me too passive an emotion for this violent, dramatic poem which may have been composed in a trance, like some others. In the Koran (28:80) Korah was an arrogant rich man who was eventually swallowed up by the earth. The reference to opium here might be real or metaphorical.

146 F1472. D2–103. Line 5. An unusual autobiographical touch.

147 F2973. Not traced in D.

148 F304. D304. Lines 1–10. A rebeck (Arabic/Farsi *rebāb*) is a stringed instrument like a viol played with a bow. *To God is the returning:* Koran 2:156.

149 F2831. D2–1466. Lines 1–7. His sense of direction towards Mecca, the *qiblē*, should be provided by the *mehrāb*, a niche in the mosque wall. This couplet is omitted in Kadkani's edition, for no apparent reason.

150 F1331. D1–1338. Line 1. The Farsi word *rang* used here has connotations which go well beyond its basic meaning of colour, suggesting quality or characteristic.

151 F412. D417. Lines 1–4.

152 F911. D1–915. N XXIV. I have translated *lā makān* as placeless again in the final line.

153 F3053. D2–1688. Line 8. I have picked out this line because Rumi himself quotes it in *Fihi Ma Fihi*. The verb *shemordan* means to count or reckon as, and the sense here is to be comparable to i.e. as real or solid as the body.

154 The last of my interpolations, intended to help focus the text near its conclusion. See *inter alia* No 111. The divine injunction 'Be!' (6:72; 36:82) encompassed the whole of creation, and the mystery of being (see F631, F940) is arguably the core theme of the *Divan*, and one which goes well beyond the idea of human being, to signal that which is both limitless and eternal, erasing the boundary between self and other. Rumi uses two words, the Arabic *vojūd* which means something like everyday life or ordinary existence, and the Persian *hasti* which is the noun from the verb to be. The sense of the latter varies but it sometimes denotes 'being' in its deepest sense. Rumi's search for essence is also revealed in his use of the formula 'the X of the X of the X' (see for example No 52). Western readers may find Heidegger's distinction between existence and being, as set out in *Being and Time*, relevant here.

155 F1716. D2–347. Line 8. The notion of being is often contrasted with *'adam* which can be translated as non-being, non-existence, or as here, nothingness. It is a highly complex concept referring sometimes to the state of things before God brought the world into being, and sometimes to post-existence, i.e. death. But it is not entirely negative, and to my mind has some affinities with the Buddhist notion of the void, which paradoxically can be generative. This couplet is from a ghazal which pivots on the contrast between being and non-being, but which I found too disjunctive to translate as a whole. In the second line Chittick (1983:320) translates the word *tars* in the usual way as fear whereas Schimmel (1978:242) omits it altogether. I think the sense is rather of nervous anticipation: he wants to be swept away but is equally afraid of losing his identity. A conflict which both lovers and mystics may experience. See also No 36. For a discussion of annihilation (*fanā*) of the self (*nafs*) through love see Zarrabi-Zadeh (2014).

156 F327. D327. In the first Persian line the phrase *ghairat-e lotf* literally means something like 'kindly zeal' although *ghairat* is a complex word which can also mean jealousy or envy (see Chittick, 1983: 304–5). Likewise in English the words zealous and jealous have a common root in the ancient Greek *zelos*, which in turn derives from the verb to boil, and there is also apparently a common root in ancient Hebrew. Thus there is disagreement about the wording of Exodus 34:14: 'for the Lord ... is a jealous/zealous God'. I have used 'deliverance' here which not only has powerful religious connotations of divine agency (e.g. 'deliver us from evil') but which is sometimes used of death after a period of suffering, which seems to me the sense here. The first line is the last line of a ghazal in the Discourses of Shams (Chittick, 2004:138.)

157 F *tarj'iāt* 10 line 9. D *tarj'iāt* 1 (unnumbered) line 9. From the appendix of strophe poems.

158 F1789. D2-423. N XXXVI. Lines 1-6. This is an example of another conventional theme in Persian (and Arabic) poetry, that of the departing caravan. The word *sabuk* literally means light but here I think has the sense of superficial or trivial. Here I have translated *lā makān* as the 'emptiness the void' to get both the physical sense of the desert and spiritual sense of nothingness. As will have become obvious by now, Rumi frequently uses the exclamatory 'O' (the very similar *ei* in Farsi) both at the beginning and in the middle of poems. Interestingly this long, open vowel sound, or something like it, exists as an exclamation or invocation in a number of European languages, for example in the 19th century French symbolist poet Rimbaud's famous '*Ô saisons! O châteaux*!' (O seasons! O castles!). One wonders if there was some basic Indo-European root of this kind which over time became voiced in a range of languages. Arabic, which belongs to a different linguistic family, does not have a similar sound.

159 F903. D1-907. Line 6.

160 F683. D1-687. The speech from the tomb is another conventional theme in Persian poetry. The notion of drunken ecstasy which goes beyond reason and the intellect gets one of its strongest expressions here.

TEXT AND CONTEXT

The Persian language (Farsi) has changed remarkably little over the centuries. There have been some minor grammatical shifts and a few letters are pronounced differently now from the way they were in the past. Of course some words have fallen out of use and many new ones come in. But the modern Iranian reader can still understand without too much difficulty the welcome to spring of the 9th/10th century poet Rūdaki:

āmad bahār-e khorram bā rang o buye teib
ba sad hezār zīnnat o ārāyesh-e ajīb

Spring came
with colors and scents
a hundred thousand trimmings
and strange get-up
(Squires, 1998: 466-67)

It is not just that modern Iranians still have direct access to one of the golden ages of world literature, a legacy that may actually have helped to stabilise the language over time. It is the range and variety of such poetry that is astonishing. If they want a national epic they have Ferdowsi's *Book of Kings*. If they want a spiritual allegory they have Attār's *Chronicle of the Birds*. If they want exemplary language or peerless lyricism they have Sa'di and Hāfez. If they prefer neat existential reflections they have Khayyām (without Fitzgerald's languor). For epic romances they have Nezāmi. There are panegyric odes on the one hand and biting satire on the other. And mysticism? A sense of the mystery of life pervades a good deal of Persian poetry and various names come to mind including one mentioned in a ghazal in this book, that of Rumi's predecessor, Sanā'i. Jāmi would come later. But it is Rūmi (1207-73) who towers above all others.

Rumi's fame rests on three main works: the *Masnavi*, a long poem comprising a mixture of stories, sermons and spiritual reflections; the *Divān-e Shams*, a collection of over three thousand ghazals and several hundred quatrains; and a collection of discourses gnomically entitled *Fīhi mā Fīhi* (literally 'in it is what is in it)'. Any attempt to grasp Rumi's thinking requires some familiarity with all three. However, the second, which is sometimes called the *Divān-e Kabīr* (the great collection) offers on its own a powerful and more personal insight into his life and thought, and it is thus not surprising that this has been thoroughly edited in Persian and quite widely translated in the West.

As was noted in the Preface, the *Divan* is largely though not wholly about the meeting between Rumi and Shams, and can be read as an account of that friendship. However, although this relationship has its personal dimension, it was fundamentally a spiritual encounter. Some Western readers initially saw this passionate story of two men in homosexual terms, and perhaps some still do, but this is to misunderstand the nature of it. Pederasty was a common feature of Persian courts at the time, and clearly existed in other contexts also; witness Rumi's scathing comment about people who wear the (Sufi) woollen robe, patch it, and commit sodomy (see Chittick, 1983: 190). And in the Discourses he speaks at one point about being in love with a boy (Arberry, 1961:108 has 'youth') or a woman (Thackston, 1994: 100; see also p. 167). But as both the Discourses and the *Divan* make clear, following the Koran, carnal lust was seen as something to be overcome in the process of spiritual development (Thackston, 1994: 63-4: Koran 79:40-

41). It is perhaps difficult for us now to understand how such a relationship could be so close but not expressed in physical terms (and some of Rumi's followers probably thought so too) but the relationship between the Sufi master (sheikh or elder) and his followers could be just as intense in other ways. To comprehend this, we need to say something briefly about Shams and then about Sufism.

The *Maqālāt* or Discourses of Shams (Chittick, 2004; Fouchécour, 2017) give us a real insight into this complex and charismatic figure. By turns harsh and gentle, orthodox and scandalous, he clearly exercised a powerful fascination on those he met, attracting some and alienating others. He had no time for fools and even sometimes friends. He was spontaneous and unpredictable, quoting the dictum that a Sufi was a 'son of the moment'. He stood for the gaze of love rather than the gaze of knowledge, preferring Plato to Avicenna for that reason. Clearly, Rumi was bowled over, personally and spiritually, but at one point Shams says revealingly that while he and Rumi saw the beauty in each other, Rumi did not see the ugliness in him. He has enormous respect and love for Rumi but perhaps thinks that the latter treats him with more respect than he deserves. It is a dynamic, shifting, turbulent but deeply rewarding spiritual relationship in which Shams comes across as a dangerous truth-teller, challenging all that he saw as lazy, anodyne or hypocritical. In this, he was typical of the wilder shores of Sufism.

Sufism was and remains a very complex and diverse subject and only a few basic points will be made here. Pointers to the extensive literature on it are given below. It is usually described as the mystical tradition within Islam, although in modern times it has appealed to people outside that religion also. In terms of the theological debate within Islam about the relationship between reason and revelation Sufism is associated with the latter and was indeed rather hostile to ratiocination. It was much more widespread and salient in Rumi's time than it is now, and there was a variety of orders, ranging from the socially respectable to the highly unconventional. That said, many more orthodox Muslims regarded Sufism with a degree of suspicion and sometimes hostility. (I am using 'orthodox' here not as a precise religious term but simply to refer broadly to the basic, consensual beliefs of Muslims, whether Sunni or Shia.) Islam is a religion of strict observance and Sufis—especially the less conventional ones—seemed to ignore the rules. The unorthodox nature of Sufism has sometimes been attributed to the absorption of non-Islamic influences, especially Greek gnosticism, and this is not impossible since Muslim scholarship in the early centuries was very wide-ranging and included the translation of many Greek texts. However, modern scholars have mostly discounted this view and Sufis themselves have argued that there was a firm basis in the Koran and the sayings attributed to the Prophet (*hadith*, pl. *ahādith*) for their beliefs and practices, and the pursuit of an 'inner way'. Thus grew up a whole vocabulary and tradition of hidden meanings and esoteric interpretation. The Koran is after all a divine revelation and so the idea of pursuing that to deeper levels seemed to them wholly justifiable, even necessary. Those who took a more literal view regarded such interpretation as unnecessary and even dangerous.

Here, it may be useful to take a step back. Christian theology draws a distinction between God as transcendent and God as immanent. We must be very cautious about applying ideas developed in one religious context to another, but the distinction may be helpful in understanding the issue here. A transcendent God is one that is wholly beyond the human compass. Strictly speaking the phrase *allāhu akbar* should be translated not as 'God is great' but 'God is greater': greater than anything we can possibly conceive of or imagine (the adjective *akbar* is the comparative or superlative of *kabīr*). This is the view of God which the Koran projects: 'Nothing resembles him.' (42:11). However, the Koran also contains verses which point to or at least allow a view of God as immanent, to be found deep within our selves or souls (41: 52). One of these verses—'We are nearer to him than his jugular vein' (50:16) is quoted in one of the ghazals here. And in the Discourses Rumi also expands on the favourite Sufi *hadith* (saying) that he who knows himself knows his Lord (Thackston, 1994: 11; see also Chittick, 2004: 357 in relation to Shams) although the authenticity of this is contested. Sufis saw, and still see, such statements as the basis for their pursuit of the inner or hidden way.

The most famous or notorious statement of immanence was the claim of the iconic Sufi al-Hallaj (referred to in the *Divan* by his first name Mansūr): *ana al-haq*. The Arabic word *haq* is difficult to translate: the noun *haqiqat* means 'reality' but in ordinary conversation '*haq dārīd*' simply means 'you are right'. The term thus denotes Reality or Truth in both their everyday and their strongest senses, and it is one of the 99 names of God. Hallaj was taken to be claiming that he was God, and was subsequently executed for blasphemy. Rumi refers to this in several ghazals. What Sufis focussed on however was the word 'I' (*ana*). For them, this was not the usual, everyday subject, the ego or self, but the deep, inner ground of being, to be reached only through the abandonment of the everyday self in mystical practice.

Such mystical practice equally involved the rejection of reason and the intellect and a questioning of language itself. For most people this would have been a major step, but for Rumi, such rejection and questioning involved turning his whole life upside down. He had, after all, been a learned and well-respected religious scholar for many years, steeped in the complexities of Islamic theology which had evolved over centuries of careful deliberation. Through his family background, he was already well versed in Sufism but nothing could prepare him for his encounter with Shams, who was at the radical end of the Sufi spectrum. Their meeting was to prove traumatic, exhilarating and life-changing.

The rejection of reason and moderation meant embracing their opposites, emotion and excess. (I once was invited to attend a large Sufi gathering in Isfahan, where I was the only foreigner. There were readings of religious texts and some chanting and a great outpouring of emotion and weeping. I also made an unforgettable winter journey to visit the Ne'matollāhi shrine in the small village of Mahan near Kerman.) The language of Sufism reflects this dismissal of reason and the *Divan* is no exception. However, we need to be careful in how we interpret it, since some of it is metaphorical. Drunkenness refers not to an alcohol-induced stupor but to the kind of loss of inhibition and control that drunkards exhibit. Likewise, madness refers not to clinical insanity but to loss of rationality. It is possible that some of the wilder Sufis—the *qalandars*—did drink wine in their quest to break all the taboos, and equally some devotees probably lost their minds. But the underlying meaning of such metaphors is the loss of self, the *ek-stasis* or standing outside the self—ecstasy—that is central to many mystical traditions. While Sufis sometimes deliberately provoked censure (*malāmatīye*) as a way of challenging and exposing the prevailing societal conventions (and often hypocrisy or double standards) we should remember that the reason for doing this was not primarily to present a social critique but to deepen personal spirituality.

The idea of the self is also the point of departure for what is surely the central theme of the *Divan*, namely love. The common human experience of falling in love typically involves a departure from the normal self. People forget or abandon their usual tasks and routines in their absorption in the other person. In this way, many people can identify with the poetry of Rumi because it describes that 'falling'—and the word is apposite. This helps to explain why so many readers who have no knowledge of Islam have found that he speaks to them.

It is the coming together of Persian poetry with this notion of love which produces the particular, complex and multi-layered nature of Rumi's *Divan*. According to one theory (Dabāshi, 2003) Persian love poetry originated in popular, folk verse of the kind found in many cultures. However, as this gradually became adopted into aristocratic court settings, several things happened. First there was a shift of gender. What had been a male/female matter of the love between men and women became largely a masculine affair, or at least expressed in those terms in the *majles*, the exclusively male gatherings which were an occasion for discussion, performance of music and verse, food and drink and general conviviality. The caveat 'expressed' is necessary, first because Persian has the same word for he and she, so we cannot be sure. But secondly, it was or became the convention to express love in terms of relationships between men; women were excised from lyrical court poetry, although they still figured in longer romantic epics such as Leila and Majnūn. Secondly, love came to encompass love for the ruler or patron, much as one had to describe the latter as handsome or beautiful however ugly he was. Thirdly, court love poetry began to take on a spiritual or mystical tinge, giving love and loving a cosmic dimension. Dabashi regarded this as a subversion or even inversion of true love poetry but there is no doubt that much Persian lyric poetry has these various levels or aspects. If one looks up the words *ebhām* and *eihām* in the dictionary they are both translated as 'ambiguity' but while the first means ambiguity in the normal sense of either this or that, the second is vaguer and more open, indicating a kind of polyvalence, things or meanings that can go in several directions, perhaps even at the same time. It is the latter which is characteristic not just of Rumi but much other Persian lyric poetry, especially Hafez.

The sense of the Beloved in the *Divan* also seems to go well beyond the individual to that person as a locus of something much wider or deeper. We sometimes talk about the person who is loved in a way which seems to transcend their actual existence: 'you are the world to me'. And from there love can broaden and deepen to become an ontological concept, the fundamental impetus of life, of creation. One *hadith* states that God created the world in order that he should be known: 'I was a hidden treasure ...' (Thackston, 1994: 84). This implies a relationship with the knower, a relationship which may range from awe through obedience (and sometimes disobedience) to love. Both the Old Testament and the Koran have many severe passages dealing with obedience, transgression and punishment. But for Sufis the sense that creation was fundamentally an act of love requires those who were created to love in return. The Koran refers to people whom He loves and who love Him (5:54). The self is left behind in this act of devotion.

The recent popularity and popularisation of Sufism and Rumi in the west is double-edged. On the one hand it is all to the good, bringing this great mystic to an audience far beyond the confines of his original time and place. It is testimony to the universal in Rumi, his capacity to communicate with all men and women. The Western taste for Eastern mysticism began in the 19th century, as a side-effect of western colonialism, and became a more general phenomenon during the 20th, perhaps due to the pervasive materialism and technicism of our times. There is clearly an appetite for something more, something different. However, Rumi's popularity may have come at the cost of de-emphasizing his Islamic identity. While Sufism was regarded as unorthodox and even heretical by some Muslims (the idea of 'saints' or 'holy men' embraced by some Sufis is anathema to most Muslims who regard the Prophet Mohammed as the only human being worthy of veneration as the 'perfect man') there are elements in Rumi's poetry which are profoundly Islamic. One of the ghazals translated here is in praise of the fast, and there are others. The unicity of God is never in question. There are numerous references to the Koran, which Rumi was steeped in, and to the *ahādith*, the sayings attributed to the Prophet which were authenticated according to strict Islamic procedures. And prayer runs through the *Divan* like a thread to the point where, in the penultimate translation here, it has become his life.

To digress briefly: it is interesting to compare the case of Rumi with that of another of Islam's great theologians and mystics, Mohammed Al Ghazāli (1058-1111). There are both similarities and differences. Both men achieved prominence as spiritual teachers when they were still relatively young, Ghazali being appointed as chief professor at one of the most prestigious theological colleges in Baghdad. Both then experienced a sudden break or rupture in their life and work, Rumi through Shams but Ghazali in an even more dramatic way: he suddenly stopped in the middle of a lecture and could not continue speaking. He then abandoned his career and family (though making provision for them) and took on the life of a wandering dervish. It was some years before he began to teach and write again, producing some of the major theological works of his faith. In contrast, Rumi's crisis led to the great outpouring of poetry that we know. However, each made a major shift towards mysticism, and some people see Ghazali as one of the founding fathers of Sufism. Two points can be made about both of them. The fact that men of such powerful scholastic intellects largely abandoned rational thought in favour of the 'inner way' speaks volumes about the power of mysticism in those centuries. Secondly, both cases raise the issue of the adequacy of language in relation to the *mysterium*. In Ghazali's case, it led to sudden, complete silence, which was only broken over time. In Rumi's case we see the relentless pressure on language in his poetry, in the form of exclamation, repetition, paradox, hyperbole and disjunction. We often have the sense of words and prosody being pushed to their limits.

To resume: this general note can be kept brief because so much has been written about Rumi already and no attempt has been made to replicate this. Some of what follows will thus be simplified and readers who wish to can refer to the sizable literature on him, of which three books, written in different decades, stand out: Schimmel (1978), Chittick (1983) and Lewis (2000). Each of these deals with Rumi's life, beliefs and works, and contains some translations of the *Divan*. There is a wider, more popular literature also, often focussing on spiritual themes which have attracted a wider audience in the West, and especially the US. Two scholarly translations of some ghazals should be noted: Nicholson (1898; reprinted 2001) and Arberry (combined and corrected edition, 2009). There are also a number of shorter books of translations or versions, including one of the quatrains by Mafi and Kolin (2014). The Dar al Masnavi website usefully collates the numbering of various translations, including those based on the Turkish text, as well as giving translations of a small number of ghazals.

Any new book of translations thus has to be justified. In all, I estimate that only about one-fifth of the over 3000 ghazals in the *Divan* have been translated, literally or freely, into English. There thus remains an enormous task to be completed. However, this book only adds a small proportion to that total, and my motivation has been rather different. I wanted to produce translations which, while firmly grounded in the originals, were readable as poetry in English. After all, Rumi wrote them as poetry and however useful literal, prose translations are, they are not the real thing, lacking the patterning, idiom and voice of the originals. Above all, they do not capture the swirling energy of Rumi's verse which in itself constitutes a kind of dance.

At first sight this might seem a rather quixotic enterprise, not simply because of the difficulties of turning poetry in one language into that in another, but because as one ghazal makes clear, Rumi did not think much of his own poetry, comparing it to Egyptian bread which was fine when fresh but stale the next day. It is a revealing remark. This was performance poetry, usually declaimed and accompanied by or interspersed with music and sometimes together with the iconic dancing in the Mevlevi order, in a highly charged atmosphere. No wonder it seemed stale the morning after, when it had been committed to paper. As well as reading and working through the poems, I often used to just skim them. This might seem a strange and unscholarly thing to do, but it allowed me to get a sense of their dynamics, the flow and movement of the lines, the repetition of words and phrases, and the improvisation on them almost like a jazz riff. One can hear the aural logic, the way one sound leads on to another, carrying the verse forward within immense élan and drive. Rumi's poetry is not finely crafted, with the delicate interlacing and meshing that one finds in Sa'di or Hafez. The construction of the ghazals tends to be quite loose, with one theme or metaphor developed for a few couplets, then moving on to a different one. The well-known issue of 'unity' (or lack of it) in the Persian ghazal takes an acute form here, which of course creates problems for the western reader used to more linear, less disjunctive writing. However, at a deeper level, there is a basic unity in the sense that most of the ghazals are about one thing: the spiritual search. I have nevertheless sometimes translated part of a ghazal rather than the whole thing, since I judged it would make a more readable, artistically coherent poem in English. Despite this, I hope that this book as a whole reflects the range and depth of Rumi's verse.

For all the emphasis on his Sufism, we should not underestimate the extent to which Rumi inherited and was part of a poetic, literary tradition, to which he in turn contributed, influencing others after him. There are nature poems, about the seasons. There are poems about the heavens, the sun, moon and stars. There are poems about music and musicians. There are poems about travelling, the caravan and caravanserai. There are poems about the grave, the tomb. As pointed out above, Rumi also inherits the long tradition of Persian love poetry, and some of the ghazals read like any love poetry, written for any beloved. This of course complicates their interpretation and some of the ghazals in the *Divan* were not addressed to Shams or about him at all. Indeed, Rumi found further 'significant others' after Shams disappeared finally from his life.

Some of the shorter ghazals are less declamatory, quieter, more unified. These read more like the ghazals of other poets and do not suggest a spontaneous, performance context. They work better on the page perhaps because they were created on the page, and some of the best-known ones are of this kind. That said, it is important to understand that the basic unit of Persian lyric poetry was the couplet (*beyt*) rather than the line. An Iranian scholar has stated that one of Hafez' innovations was to 'give independence to the couplet' (see the discussion in Squires, 2014: 431-32). This may be true but even in Rumi the structure of self-contained couplets is often apparent. It is worth noting that unlike the European sonnet, the ghazal has no fixed length, and many of Rumi's poems are considerably longer than the ghazals of other poets. Indeed the title of *ghazal*, which means a short lyric or expressive poem (in contrast to the *qasidē* which is an ode to a particular, usually socially or politically exalted, figure) can only be loosely applied to some of the poems that comprise the *Divan*.

For readers coming new to Rumi or Persian poetry, several other features of this work should be mentioned. The first is a tradition of hyperbole, of exaggeration or over-statement- for example the unattributed lines quoted in Shams's *Maqālāt* (Fouchécour, 2017: 233, my trans.)

> If in hell your hair came into my hands
> I would take pity on those in paradise

Some of this may stem from the necessary excess of compliments paid to a king or patron, but it pervades much classical Persian verse, including Rumi. I sense there is something deeper also, a kind of aesthetic idealism or taste for perfection in the culture. That said, our perception of and reaction to hyperbole partly depends on where we are coming from. Much modern poetry is relentlessly low-key and ordinary, perhaps a reaction against the high rhetoric of earlier times. Style is always an issue for the translator and I have tried to strike a balance between the rhetoric of the original and what may be acceptable to the contemporary western reader.

A second feature is the ready use of symbolism. The name of Shams, meaning 'sun', lends itself to this, but he is also compared to the moon because of its and his beauty (whether he was beautiful or not). Wine is not just an alcoholic drink but as noted above something that allows one to transcend reason and the intellect, to lose oneself. The house is a locus for spiritual gatherings and the garden a reminder of paradise. The road is a paradigm of the Way. Sleep is a symbol of unawareness, perhaps reflecting the Islamic dawn invocation: 'prayer is better than sleep'.

Another feature is the naming of the addressee of the poem, often at the end. This practice was important in a court context both in order to acknowledge and flatter the recipient and to ensure that the destination of the poem was clear, usually in the hope of some reward. By no means all the ghazals in the *Divan* refer to Shams but many do, and some that don't seem likely to have been about him. The issue in this case was obviously not one of reward, but of respect and love.

Selecting poems to translate from such a vast corpus has been a profound problem. I was initially guided by Kadkani's selected edition which contains 466 (see Notes). I also looked at what others have translated. However, my initial choice was simply based on poems I liked and thought might work in English: poems that I could do something with. However, over time, I found two themes gradually but insistently emerging: the narrative of the relationship between Rumi and Shams, beginning with their initial meeting and ending with Shams' ultimate disappearance (which some have speculated was due to his murder by a jealous family member or follower, although there is no hard evidence for this) and the underlying, unfolding spiritual search. In the original editions, the poems are arranged alphabetically by the end of the first line, in the normal Persian way, so the order I have arrived at here is my own.

As noted above, I have translated some ghazals in their entirety, but also often extracted passages or lines from them. Indeed, as the text developed, I began to intersperse longer pieces with short excerpts, sometimes just a couplet, especially in the later stages of the book. The discontinuous nature of the ghazals allows, even encourages this, although readers may wish to compare what I have done with Arberry's or Lewis's complete translations. But I have also been prompted by the sense, rightly or wrongly, that Rumi is often simply too much: too much to take on board, to respond to as a modern western reader encountering these as written texts on the page, rather than as originally in a performance context where, among other things, the pace of presentation would have been much slower, more drawn out, interspersed with music, giving the listener a lot more time to absorb and reflect. What we have in a book like this is not what Rumi delivered to his audience in the first place, and we need to remember that difference. The advice to the reader perhaps should be not to read too much at one go, to give the poems time to settle in the ear/mind and sink in.

There is a more general issue. For all the wealth of scholarship on Rumi—and some of it has been superb—he remains a very difficult figure to grasp. It is partly a matter of quantity. The *Divan* alone contains over 3000 ghazals and several hundred quatrains, and the *Masnavi* comprises some 25,000 couplets, not to mention his other output. But it has also to do with the nature of his writing and thinking, which is complex, divergent, open-ended and reflexive. Looking back on my text now, I am aware that I have been very selective both in terms of my choice of poems and lines within them. Time and again I have picked out certain bits and left others, often instinctively, in order to arrive at a sharper focus for a poem or to give a sense of shape to the whole. Remembering my own struggle over the years I have tried to help readers get some purchase on the material, even if they then decide to reject this as wrong-headed or restrictive. However, in the end, one may ask whether 'grasp' is an appropriate notion at all, given the nature of Rumi's work and thought. This is, after all, a writer who was profoundly engaged in the mystery, in the depths of being, to the outer limits of language, so the very idea of 'understanding' him might itself be reductive. It is a thought to which I suspect Rumi himself would have been sympathetic.

At a more technical level, I have not tried to reproduce the form or prosody of the originals. Farsi and English are both Indo-European languages and thus closer than say Arabic, which belongs to a different linguistic family and has a quite different kind of grammar, with permutations based on a (mainly) triliteral root. The word order of Farsi and English does however differ, in that with Farsi the verb usually comes at the end of the sentence (SOV = subject, object, verb) whereas English is SVO. Adjectives in Farsi usually come after the noun, not before. There are other differences too, but by and large the two languages are by no means as different as, say, Irish and English, which I also translate.

However, the metrical forms of Persian poetry, which are actually formulated in Arabic (equally, English metres are classified in Graeco-Roman terms) are very complex and cannot simply be replicated in English (Elwell-Sutton, 1976). Moreover, free verse is my own natural form of writing, so I have employed this, though somewhat more patterned by rhyme and rhythm than I might use for my own work: what I sometimes call 'free verse plus'. The Persian line tends to be longer than the English pentameter, often coming out at around fourteen syllables, and the half-line is thus often the more workable unit for translation. (I have avoided the established practice of referring to lines and couplets as *hemistich* and *distich*, since this is inaccurate: the first means a half-line, the second means two, the Greek *di-*

stich, i.e. the Persian *beyt* or couplet). The many compound verbs in Farsi, coming usually at the end of the verse line, facilitate rhyme and even on occasions mono-rhyme, which help to unify the whole.

Traduire c'est trahir (to translate is to betray) the French say. The above comments suggest what may be lost, or at least altered, in translation, and the general caveat needs to be borne in mind: it is an imperfect art. But I hope that what I have done here may take its place among the many other attempts to bring across to an English-speaking audience this extraordinary writer, thinker and mystic who belonged very much to, but transcended his own time and who still speaks to us now. But speaks about what, in the end?

At this point it may be useful to draw a comparison with another great Persian poet, Hafez, whom I have also translated (Squires, 2014). Both poets raise problems of interpretation, but Rumi also raises issues of reception. These have taken several forms. According to Ergin (2006) who has translated the Turkish text of the *Divan* the Turkish government did not want to support his translation of the final, and seemingly most heretical, volume, and he was forced to find another publisher. In other cases, the reverence in which Rumi is held by some Sufis has led to a hagiographical or 'spiritually correct' approach which excludes any concerns with or insights into Rumi the man and sidelines his relationship with Shams. And the enthusiasm with which Rumi has been greeted in the west in recent decades has sometimes detached him from his historical, Islamic context, turning him into a free-floating, cosmopolitan mystic. Finally, the over-riding preoccupation with Rumi as a spiritual figure has usually though not always meant less emphasis on him as a poet, on the literary qualities of his verse and his place in the Persian poetic canon.

I said at the outset that most Iranians would name Molavi, as they call him, as their greatest mystical poet. Yet if one presented readers who had no contextual knowledge of the work with many of these poems they would probably describe them simply as love poems. And indeed they are, recounting the longing, joys, happiness, doubts, quarrels, reconciliations, separations and despair of human relationships. Rumi is without question a great love poet. However, this aspect of his work has often been overshadowed or downplayed by the emphasis on the spiritual or mystical dimension. It is only when one goes back to the poems themselves, the actual texts, that this aspect becomes clear. Indeed, those who have popularised Rumi in the West are perhaps closer to the texts in this respect than those who read him through a purely hagiographical lens. Is this a problem?

First we need to say something about the relationship between Rumi and Shams, based on the poetry of the former and the Discourses (*Maqālāt*) of the latter, in particular the invaluable thematic analysis provided in Fouchécour's translation (2017: 411-504). This relationship has puzzled scholars, so what follows here must be regarded as tentative. Although Rumi and Shams were deeply attached to each other, the relationship seems to have been asymmetrical. Shams respected and revered Rumi for his great learning and piety. Indeed, he had spent years looking for someone who had the capacity to grasp what he had to say. In that sense, Rumi was his project and when the work was complete he would move on, as he may well have done. (However Shams's final disappearance remains shrouded in mystery, and although the murder hypothesis is now largely discounted, there is no doubt that he faced great hostility from some of Rumi's family and followers). Shams's insistence that he should not be considered Rumi's *sheikh* or spiritual master (Chittick, 2004: 212ff) should be seen in this light, since that would have implied a permanent relationship and a degree of authority whereas Shams saw it as a loving, if temporary partnership. Shams claimed that when both of them were drunk on the love of God, Rumi was oblivious to the world while he remained conscious of it (Fouchécour, 2017: 79). And while the thematic analysis (*Clés de Lecture*) shows that love is an important theme in the *Maqālāt* it is by no means as dominant as it is in the *Divan* and is sometimes expressed in terms of the more temperate *hub* than passionate *'eshq* (Fouchécour, 2017: 447-9). For Rumi, however, the relationship was quite different. It is as if Shams, by his very words and presence, embodied a spirituality which touched Rumi's innermost being. It was a deeply emotional relationship. Whereas there seems to have been an element of conscious purposiveness on Shams's side, Rumi appears simply to have been captivated by this strange dervish and his insights from the start, to have been completely smitten or bowled over, much to the surprise and alarm of his followers and students and wife. The expressions are telling: they are the ones we use of love. One may love someone in various ways and for various reasons but there is no other way to describe Rumi's feelings for Shams. Those feelings are manifested most clearly in those poems where Shams is planning to leave or has already disappeared. Rumi is desolate, inconsolable. The person who meant so much to him has gone. Who does not know that feeling? But to ask again: is this a problem?

The relationship between the human and the spiritual may be a problem for two kinds of audience. In the west, human love and divine love may seem quite different to many people, and they can find it difficult to see a bridge between them, much less cross it. Of course the metaphor of human love is there in some parts of the Christian tradition; witness the notion of the church as the bride of Christ. However, one senses a certain uneasiness about this linking of the human and physical with the divine. I noted in my book on Hafez that whereas the word 'beauty' occurs quite frequently in the Old Testament, it does not occur once in the New. Perhaps the human-divine link is stronger in the Jewish tradition, going back to the Song of Solomon. In secular literature, one does sometimes find such a link. Proust in *Time Regained* speaks of the divinity of which people are fragmentary reflections

(1972: 267). However, it is arguably not a central theme in western literature, at least not in modern times.

The aspect of human love in Rumi may also be a problem for some Muslim readers, as it was in the case of another poet, philosopher and mystic, ibn Arabi (Nicholson, 1911). Orthodox Islam holds firmly to the view that only God is worthy of adoration, and that to bestow that on anyone or anything else is idolatry. Some Persian poets, including Rumi, consistently and provocatively use the word *bot* (idol) to describe the beloved, and this is one thing that separates Sufis from their more orthodox co-religionists. Whereas the latter see the love or adoration of human beings as potentially a distraction or even impediment to love of the divine, many Sufis see the *bot* as a valid and even necessary step along the way. The veneration of the *sheikh* or *pīr,* the spiritual elder, is likewise part of the Sufi tradition but often rejected as impious outside it. But as noted earlier we often revert to quasi-religious language when expressing human love: 'he worships the ground she stands on', 'she adores him'; and so on.

In the banality of these ordinary statements lies a profound truth. Love, of all kinds, involves a going out of the self, a movement away from the ego, towards the beloved other, a giving up or abnegation or surrender. And it is perhaps above all in that sense of the abandonment, the leaving behind of the controlling or centred self that the real message of Rumi lies, whether it is interpreted in human or divine terms, or both.

SELECT BIBLIOGRAPHY

Given the wealth of existing literature on Rumi (see in particular the many sources in Lewis, 2000) and on Sufism (see among others the work of William Chittick, Carl Ernst and the late Leonard Lewisohn) this bibliography has been confined to those works which bear directly on these translations. For those who are interested, the bibliography in my book of Hafez translations lists more general references on Persian literature and culture.

The *Mawlana Rumi Review*, published annually, contains articles, translations and reviews.

Encyclopaedia Iranica is an invaluable source of articles on a wide range of subjects including not only Rumi (multiple authors) but for example Hallaj, Ahmad and Mohammad Ghazali, Ebn Al-Arabi (Ibn Arabi), Sana'i, dervishes (*darvīsh*), hadith, the ghazal and even hyperbole. It is easier to access the Encyclopaedia first and then follow the internal index. Not all articles are available online and the enormous project is still in progress.

Abdul Hakim, K. (1965) *The Metaphysics of Rumi*. Lahore: Institute of Islamic Culture.

Al 'Arabi, M. ibn (1911) *The tarjumān al-ashwāq: a collection of mystical odes* (trans. R.A. Nicholson). London: Royal Asiatic Society.

Anvar-Chenderoff, L. (2004). *Rūmī*. Paris: Entrelacs.

Arberry, A. J. (1961) *Discourses of Rumi*. London: John Murray.

Arberry, A. J. (2009) *Mystical Poems of Rumi* (revised and corrected edition). Chicago: University of Chicago Press.

Barks, C. with John Moyne, A. J. Arberry and Reynold Nicholson (2004)

Rumi: selected poems. London: Penguin. First published as *The Essential Rumi* in the USA by HarperCollins Publishers 1995.

Chittick, W. C. (1983) *The Sufi Path of Love: the spiritual teachings of Rumi*. Albany: State University of New York Press.

Chittick, W. C. (2004) *Me and Rumi: the autobiography of Shams-i Tabrizi*. Louisville: Fons Vitae.

Dabāshi, H. (2003) It was in China late one moonless night, *Social Research*, 70(3), 935-980, Fall 2003.

Darr, R. A. H. (2014) Rumi and individuality, *Mowlana Rumi Review*, 5: 73-87.

Darvīsh, M. (1352) *kolliāt-e divān-e shams-e tabrīzī* (chāp-e sevvum). Single volume/two parts. Tehran: javidan.

De Bruijn, J. T. P. (1997) *Persian Sufi Poetry: an introduction to the mystical use of classical poems*. Richmond: Curzon.

de Vitray-Meyerovitch, E. and Mokri, M. (1973) *Odes Mystiques (Dīvān-e Shams-e Tabrīzī)*. Paris: Editions Klincksieck.

Elwell-Sutton, L. P. (1976) *The Persian Metres*. Cambridge: Cambridge University Press.

Ergin, N. O. and Johnson, W. (2006) *The Forbidden Rumi: the suppressed poems of Rumi on love, heresy and intoxication*. Rochester, Vermont: Inner Traditions.

Forūzānfar, B. (1363) *kolliāt-e shams yā divān-e kabīr* (chāp-e sevvum). Tehran: sepehr. Nine volumes/ten parts.

Fouchécour, C-H. (2017) *La Quête du Joyau: paroles inouïes de Shams, maître de Jalāl al-din Rūmi*. Paris: Cerf.

Lewis, F. D. (2000) *Rumi: past and present east and west*. Oxford: Oneworld.

Lewis, F. D. (2008) *Rumi: Swallowing the Sun: poems translated from the Persian*. Oxford: Oneworld.

Lewis, F. (2014) Towards a chronology of the poems in the Dīvān-i Shams:

a prolegomenon for a periodization of Rumi's literary oeuvre, in Lewisohn, op.cit., loc. 3288.

Lewisohn, L. (ed.) (2014) *The Philosophy of Ecstacy: Rumi and the Sufi tradition.* Bloomington, Ind.: World Wisdom.

Mafi, M. and Kolin, M. (2014) *Rumi's Little Book of Love.* San Antonio: Hierophant.

Nicholson, R. A. (1914) *The Mystics of Islam.* London: Routledge and Kegan Paul.

Nicholson, R. A. (1964) *The Idea of Personality in Sufism.* Lahore: Sh. Muhammad Ashraf.

Nicholson, R. A. (2001) *Selected Poems from the Divan-e Shams-e Tabrizi of Jalaluddin Rumi.* Bethesda: Ibex.

Proust, M. (1972) *Time Regained* (trans. Andreas Mayor). London: Chatto and Windus.

Rawan Farhadi, A. G. (2010) The human beloved and the divine beloved in the poetry of Mawlana Rumi, *Mawlana Rumi Review*, 1: 100-107.

Shafi'i-Kadkani, M. R. (1974) *gozīde-ye ghazaliyāt-e shams.* Tehran: sherkate sahami-ye ketābhāye jībī in association with Franklin Book Programs Inc.

Schimmel, A. (1978) *The Triumphal Sun: a study of the works of Jalaluddin Rumi.* London: Fine Books.

Schimmel, A. (1982) *As through a Veil: mystical poetry in Islam.* Oxford: Oneworld.

Squires, G. (1998) Translations from the Persian in: Washburn, K. and Major, J. S. (eds) *World Poetry.* New York: Norton, pp 466-67.

Squires, G. (2014) *Hafez: translations and interpretations of the ghazals.* Oxford, Ohio: Miami University Press.

Thackston, W. M. jr. (1994) *Signs of the Unseen: the Discourses of Jalaluddin Rumi.* Boston: Shambhala.

Zarrabi-Zadeh, S. (2014) Jalāl al-Dīn Rumi's mysticism of love-based annihilation, *Mawlana Rumi Review*, 5: 26-72.

For a translation of the Koran I have mostly used *The Qur'an: a new translation* by Tarif Khalidi, Penguin Classics, London, 2008, although I have consulted and sometimes referred to other translations as well.

My main Persian-English dictionary has been Steingass, F. (1892, reprinted 1970) *A Comprehensive Persian-English Dictionary*, Beirut: Librairie du Liban. For Persian-Persian dictionaries I have used the online version of Dehkhodā's *loghat nāmē*, and Anvari's *farhang-e feshurde-ye sokhan*.

ACKNOWLEDGEMENTS

I was a Lecturer in English Language and Literature in the Faculty of Letters, later to become University of Isfahan from 1964–67. It was during that time that I first became acquainted with the poetry of Rumi and these translations repay a long-term debt to the friends and students who introduced me to his work then. When my Hafez translations appeared in 2014, one of the latter, Moh Ghanoonparvar, who by then was Emeritus Professor of Persian and Comparative Literature in the University of Texas at Austin, contacted me again. Since then we have enjoyed a very fruitful collaboration and I am profoundly grateful for the care with which he has gone through my text, making many useful comments. I am also beholden to the eminent French scholar Charles-Henri de Fouchécour for our discussions over the years and for sending me a copy of his superb translation of Shams' *Maqālāt.* I gained a great deal from the conference on Rumi's poetry organised by the Iran Heritage Foundation and the British Museum in 2008. My thanks also go to Ahmad Boroumand for his help in obtaining textual materials from Iran and to Elham Shayegh for proofreading the Notes. My wife Mary has lived with my struggles with Rumi for a long time and her continued support and perceptive comments have been crucial.

Notwithstanding all this, the responsibility for the text remains my own.

Keith Tuma and his team brought this complex book into the world with loving care. Finally, I would like to thank Golnaz Fathi for her generous permission to use one of her paintings (*Untitled*, acrylic on canvas, 2007) as cover for the book, as indeed she did with another painting for my previous book of Hafez translations. It has been my great good fortune to find an Iranian painter who not only was happy to contribute to these projects but whose images seem so right for these two great poets. She may be a modern artist but her paintings are testimony to the enduring profundity and continuity of Persian culture.

GEOFFREY SQUIRES

HULL 2019

JALAL-UDDIN RUMI (1207–73) is widely regarded as the greatest of Persia's mystical poets. He was born near Balkh in Afghanistan but subsequently moved through Iran, Iraq and Syria to Konya in Turkey where he and his family found refuge from the invading Mongols. There he acquired a reputation as a pious and profound scholar and teacher but his life was turned upside down by a meeting with a wandering dervish, Shams-e Tabrizi, who challenged many of his ideas and practices. His relationship with, and ultimate separation from, Shams found expression in the thousands of lyrical and mystical ghazals in the *Divan-e Shams-e Tabrizi*, a selection of which have been translated in this book. He is best known for his didactic, mystical masterpiece, the *Masnavi*, and his teachings live on in Turkey through the Mevlevi mystical order and more widely through other Sufi organizations and his works both in Persian and in translation.

GEOFFREY SQUIRES (b.1942) is an Irish poet who was educated at the Universities of Cambridge and Edinburgh. After living and working in various countries, including three years in Iran, he settled in England and is now retired and living in Yorkshire. His poetry has been collected in *Untitled and other Poems* (2004) and *Abstract Lyrics and other Poems* (2012) both published by Wild Honey Press, Bray, Ireland. Five volumes of his poetry have recently been published in bilingual editions by Editions Unes, Nice, France. His translations of selected ghazals of the great Persian lyric poet Hafez, also published by Miami University Press, was awarded the 2014 Lois Roth annual translation prize of the American Institute of Iranian Studies. He has also published translations of early Irish poetry 600–1200 (*My News for You*, Shearsman Books, Bristol, UK, 2015).